Also by Sarah Ruhl

Plays

Passion Play: a cycle

The Clean House and Other Plays

Melancholy Play

Late: a cowboy song

Eurydice

Dead Man's Cell Phone

In the Next Room, or the vibrator play

Orlando

Stage Kiss

Dear Elizabeth: A Play in Letters from Elizabeth Bishop to Robert Lowell and Back Again

100 Essays I Don't Have Time to Write

* * * * * * * * * * * * * * * * * * * *

100 ESSAYS I DON'T HAVE TIME TO WRITE

* * * * * * * * * * * * * * * *

On Umbrellas and Sword Fights,

Parades and Dogs, Fire Alarms,

Children, and Theater

* * * * * * * * * * * * * * * *

SARAH RUHL

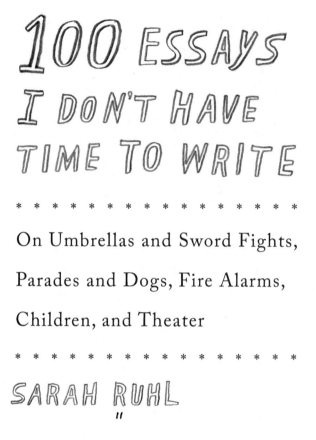

ff

Faber and Faber, Inc.

An affiliate of Farrar, Straus and Giroux   New York

Faber and Faber, Inc.
An affiliate of Farrar, Straus and Giroux
18 West 18th Street, New York 10011

Some of the essays in this book originally appeared, in slightly different form, in the following publications: "Is playwriting teachable?: the example of Paula Vogel" in the September/October 2013 issue of *The Dramatist* and *The Brown Reader* (2014); "On community theater" in *The Play That Changed My Life* (2009); and "On the loss of sword fights" in the September/October 2009 issue of *The Dramatist*.

Library of Congress Cataloging-in-Publication Data
Ruhl, Sarah, 1974– author.
    [Essays. Selections]
    100 essays I don't have time to write : on umbrellas and sword fights, parades and dogs, fire alarms, children, and theater / Sarah Ruhl.
       pages   cm
    ISBN 978-0-86547-814-5 (hardback) —
ISBN 978-0-374-71197-9 (e-book)
    I. Title.

PS3618.U48 A6 2014
814'.6—dc23

                                             2014008668

Designed by Abby Kagan

Faber and Faber, Inc., books may be purchased for educational, business, or promotional use. For information on bulk purchases, please contact the Macmillan Corporate and Premium Sales Department at 1-800-221-7945, extension 5442, or write to specialmarkets@macmillan.com.

www.fsgbooks.com
www.twitter.com/fsgbooks • www.facebook.com/fsgbooks

10   9   8   7   6   5   4   3   2   1

For my mother, Kathy Ruhl,
who taught me that the etymology
of the word essay *is* to try.

More than in any other human relationship, overwhelmingly more, motherhood means being instantly interruptible, responsive, responsible. Children need one *now* . . . It is distraction, not meditation, that becomes habitual; interruption, not continuity. —TILLIE OLSEN, *Silences*

I guess I don't really like solitude. The fun is hammering bits of it out of a crowded life.

—ROBERT LOWELL, from a letter to Elizabeth Bishop

I wanted to make something. I wanted to finish my own sentences. —LOUISE GLÜCK

Contents

Part One: On Writing Plays

Part Two: On Acting in Plays

Part Three: On People Who Watch Plays:
Audiences and Experts

Part Four: On Making Plays with Other People:
Designers, Dramaturgs, Directors, and Children

Part One

* * * * * * * * * * * * * * * * * * *

On Writing Plays

1. On interruptions

I remember reading Alice Walker's essay in my twenties about how a woman writer could manage to have one child, but more was difficult. At the time, I pledged to have no more than one, or at the very most two. (I now have three.) I also remember, before having children, reading Tillie Olsen, who described with such clarity: thinking and ironing and thinking and ironing and writing while ironing and having many children—she herself had four. I myself do not iron. My clothes and the clothes of my children are rumpled. The child's need, so pressing, so consuming, for the mother to *be there*, to be present, and the pressing need of the writer to be half-there, to be there but thinking of other things, caught me—

Sorry. In the act of writing that sentence, my son, William, who is now two, came running into my office crying and asking for a fake knife to cut his fake fruit. So there is also, in observing children much of the day and making theater much of the night, this preoccupation with the real and the illusory, and the pleasures and pains of both.

In any case, please forgive the shortness of these essays; do imagine the silences that came between—the bodily fluids, the tears, the various shades of—

In the middle of that sentence my son came in and sat at my elbow and said tenderly, "Mom, can I poop here?" I think of Virginia Woolf's *A Room of One's Own* and how it needs a practical addendum about locks and bolts and soundproofing.

But I digress. I could lie to you and say that I intended to write something totalizing, something grand. But I confess that I had a more humble ambition—to preserve for myself, in rare private moments, some liberty of thought. Perhaps that is equally 7.

My son just typed 7 on my computer.

There was a time, when I first found out I was pregnant with twins, that I saw only a state of conflict. When I looked at theater and parenthood, I saw only war, competing loyalties, and I thought my writing life was over. There were times when it felt as though my children were annihilating me (truly you have not lived until you have changed one baby's diaper while another baby quietly vomits on your shin), and finally I came to the thought, All right, then, annihilate me; that other self was a fiction anyhow. And then I could breathe. I could investigate the pauses.

I found that life intruding on writing was, in fact, life.

And that, tempting as it may be for a writer who is also a parent, one must not think of life as an intrusion. At the end of the day, writing has very little to do with writing, and much to do with life. And life, by definition, is not an intrusion.

2. Umbrellas on stage

Why are umbrellas so pleasing to watch on stage? The illusion of being outside and being under the eternal sky is created by a real object. A metaphor of limitlessness is created by the very real limit of an actual umbrella indoors. Cosmology is brought low by the temporary shelter of the individual against water. The sight of an umbrella makes us want to feel both wet and dry: the presence of rain, and the dryness of shelter. The umbrella is real on stage, and the rain is a fiction. Even if there are drops of water produced by the stage manager, we know that it won't really rain on us, and therein lies the total pleasure of theater. A real thing that creates a world of illusory things.

I have an umbrella with a picture of the sky inside. My daughter Anna said, when she was three and underneath it, "We have two skies, the umbrella sky and the real sky." When I went out with her in the rain recently without an umbrella, she said, "It's all right, Mama. I will be your umbrella." And she put her arms over my head.

3. On the loss of sword fights

We lost sword fights sometime when we lost swords. But our primal bloodlust still seems to require a good fight on stage. It's one thing to fight with our bodies and swords (it requires skill) and another to merely bicker. The gunfight on stage will not do; it will not do because it has no virtuosity and because we all know guns are fake on stage, so there is no real fear. Conversely, swords have a reality on stage even if they are fake. Fake swords make a better sound than fake guns for one thing; the sounds come from the object itself rather than a sound cue.

Shakespearean sword fights became in the nineteenth century Hedda having to bicker with her husband and shoot herself off stage. Theatrical death by gun trumped death by language; gun wounds are final, they do not inspire soliloquies. As for the duel . . . fake swords are mano a mano, whereas fake guns are merely, Did you remember to bring your gun or didn't you? Of course there is the matter of the quickness of the draw, but that is better captured on film than on the stage.

Perhaps people go to the movies instead of theaters today because their bloodlust is more accurately satisfied at the movies. Movie gunfights really do inspire fear and anxiety—as do car chases. But large-scale gunfights and car chases are no good on stage. Should actors then be trained in karate or some other fighting art? Should they be trained in physical fighting rather than in the art of the verbal duel? And if all actors were trained combatants, how would it affect our writing? Would our writing grow more teeth? More muscle? More blood?

4. On titles—comedy and tragedy

Tragedy is often named for the tragic person—*King Lear*, *Hamlet*, *Julius Caesar*—whereas comedies draw from the world at large—*As You Like It*, *The Comedy of Errors*, *A Midsummer Night's Dream*. Tragedy has proper nouns, and comedy has regular old nouns that signify the world and the structure of the world over and above the individual. Is this because tragedies are about the loss of one individual soul? The tragic perspective privileges one person over the continuity of the system, whereas comedies (which often end in marriage) use linguistic structures that describe life in general persisting after the play is over. You can still "like it" after *As You Like It*, but after *Hamlet*, Hamlet is dead forever, keeps dying, keeps on being dead.

5. On titles with participles

Many titles of plays, movies, and novels these days use participles or gerunds. For example, *Leaving Las Vegas*, *Remembering Ernest Hemingway*. It would be crass for me merely to say that I have a prejudice against these participle titles, even though it would be true. It is perhaps more interesting to think about why we are in a land of the perpetual present, with no action having happened or about to happen. It is happening, unfolding, all the time, with no subject! What of these alternative titles: "I Left Las Vegas" or "I Remember Ernest Hemingway" or quite simply "Las Vegas." *I Remember Mama* would now be called "Remembering Mama." *As You Like It* would be "Liking It." Was Beckett the first participle giant with *Waiting for Godot*? But Beckett was specifically looking at the act of the participle, the act of waiting; it was not incidental, or in vogue. Plus it is in French, and doesn't that make all the difference? In French you have that little *"En"*—*"In"* Waiting for Godot." If we are "in" waiting as opposed to just waiting, we are at least located. More nouns and fewer participles! More event and more nouns, and less becoming out of time.

6. On titles and paintings

I often long to call my plays something like "Untitled #3" or "Red #4." I tend to feel neutral and utilitarian about titles, favoring nouns. However, theater is a different medium from painting, and we don't call our plays "Untitled." How is painting different from theater, and why does theater require that titles have content instead of numbers? Is a nameless play somehow not a play? Beckett occasionally called his plays things like "Rough for Theater 1" and "Rough for Theater 2." Sonnets we often call "Sonnet." Dances can be similarly untitled. In the theater do we object to the idea that a playwright might be working on a series? Or are titles simply devices to try to get people to come to the theater, in which case "Untitled" does not help? And what titles make people want to come to the theater and why do people want to come to the theater anyway and would people come to untitled works or would they be too hard to list in the newspaper? A lack of a title implies a lack of a decision and I suppose a lack of drama insofar as drama requires decisiveness. I would be interested in seeing a short series of plays, all called "Untitled." So that the eye might be redirected and the play might become ever more interior and private, with no recourse to a title that might restrict meaning. Titles by their nature imply that the play's architecture is like a bull's-eye (and some are) with the point being in the center. Sometimes the point is in the margins, or in the experience of throwing the dart.

7. On Andy Goldsworthy, theatrical structure, and the male orgasm

I am inspired by Andy Goldsworthy's outdoor sculptures. Like a playwright, he spends his time structuring decay. In his case, the natural world destroys the form, whereas in the theater, time itself and the audience's movement through time destroy the form. Structure implies subtraction or repression; without the taking away or the hiding, there is everything, or formlessness. Goldsworthy documents how already structured nature is by using subtraction and repetition. He complicates what is natural and what is artifice by pointing to already existing natural forms.

Different plays have different shapes—spheres, rectangles, wavy lines, and of course the ever-discussed and ubiquitous arc. How will we find our own natural forms in the sense of the elemental, and when should we be suspicious of the word *natural*? The playwright Mac Wellman has his students draw the structure of their plays, encouraging them to draw wiggly lines, circles, or vases, as the structure demands. Aristotle thought form was natural, but he thought the natural form was always an arc.

I remember once hearing a young male student describe the structure of his play. He said, "Well, first it starts out, then it speeds up, and it's going and it's going, and then bam, it's over." And I thought, Do we think the arc is a natural structure because of the structure of the male orgasm?

8. Don't send your characters to reform school

Sometimes I think that American dramaturgy is based not on Aristotle's *Poetics* but instead on *The Pilgrim's Progress* . . . that is to say, what has your character *learned*, how has she *changed*, what is her *journey*? All of these questions belong to a morality play. I love medieval morality plays because they are undisguised. And yet realism in the grips of a morality play is a strange genre to me—a morality play disguised as realism seems fake.

The pilgrims who founded our country *hated* the theater. (Have you ever wondered why Boston does not have a reputation for being a theater town? Which is perhaps not fair.) The pilgrim view of theater is that its only function is moral purgation.

But try applying the generic question "How complete is his or her journey?" or "What did Godot learn from having waited?" to Beckett. The questions fall short of illuminating the play.

And so I say: don't make your play into a reform school.
Don't send your characters away.

9. Should characters have last names?

The act of naming a character is sacred and mysterious. In some countries (Tibet, for example) people do not necessarily have last names. The state of having a first and last name is a cultural practice closely aligned to patriarchy, land rights, and the individuation of the self, some would say the illusion of the self. So before giving one's character a first name and a last name, one must consider whether the world one is creating on stage is a world of first and last names.

I remember once the people in a props department asked me the last name of a character in *The Clean House*. They wanted to make a hospital badge for her. I said, "You can't make a hospital badge for her because she doesn't have a last name." And they said, "Can't you make up a last name?" And I said, "No because she doesn't have a last name."

10. People in plays

The first choice any playwright must make is whether to people the play with people, as opposed to puppets, gods, voices, or inanimate objects—teacups, eggs, spoons. Mostly, this all-important choice goes unremarked upon, as it is by and large assumed that plays will have people. I suppose the choice goes unwrestled with because actors will be in our plays and we assume that actors would prefer to play people rather than stones or snails. But this is not always the case.

The finest actors, those actors with a true calling and a humble nature, might prefer to play stones or snails, or at least be willing. But it is true that some very fine actors *do* prefer to be people (rather than trees or gods or seagulls), and it is also true that many playwrights live to please actors (actors are so beautiful and have such disarmingly lovely voices, and we'd always hoped to be them, and if not to be them, then to love them from a short distance in the dark). So we want to please them, and we hope to give them the gift of people, if it is people that they want.

When I hear complaints about this writer or that writer becoming less avant-garde and more commercial, I often think that such writers actually have no active interest in the marketplace, but they do, after a time, want to please the very fine actors they work with, and they increasingly try to give such actors satisfying roles, which influences the writer's aesthetic over time, like the steady lapping of water over a rock.

And so it might be worth going back to first principles once in a while and wondering, sitting before the blank page, if one wants to people one's play with people . . . or with devils, fairies, furies, and stones.

11. An essay in praise of smallness

I admire minimalism.

12. Plays of ideas

What are plays of ideas and do they have big words in them?

The mastery of the longer-syllabled words in the English language is no doubt admirable but is not equivalent to thinking. And I do believe that thinking is an overrated medium for achieving thought.

I believe that there is often an idiomatic confusion in the phrase *play of ideas*. I think what people mean when they say a "play of ideas" is a play in which people *talk* about ideas. A talking-ideas play is different from a play where the idea is embedded in the form rather than in the conversation. It is a similar idiomatic confusion when plays are called language-driven that are actually driven by the use of large words. Some language-driven plays might use small words sparingly (Churchill or Fornes or Beckett) as the rhythm of the language is as important as the rarity or length of the words themselves. These playwrights use smallness in the service of bigness.

Small, forthright words, used in the service of condensing experience, might have an idea buried in them as large as the most expansive work that wears its intellectualism on its sleeve. The unshed tears of the deeply felt are akin to the unused large words in the service of a thought.

13. The drama of the sentence

If it is true that there is nothing new under the sun and that there are only two or three basic human stories worth telling, then the contribution of the playwright is not necessarily the story itself but the way the story is told, word for word. So that there is a drama in the linguistic progression: what word will follow what word? I might call this the drama of the sentence, how it will unfold, how it will go up and down, how it will stop.

And this drama of the sentence, of the phrase, has been largely robbed from playwrights in a culture that loves movies more than it loves poetry. In the Hollywood model (which influences the world of playwriting more and more) every person appears to be an expert of stories and shares his or her opinion with writers about how the story should go. But a writer's special purview and intimate power is how a word follows a word. And the cultural dependence on stories has slowly deprived playwrights of their province—to be the only person in the room who should know which word should follow which word, or (in Virginia Woolf's words) how a voice answers a voice. Instead, playwrights are viewed mainly as storytellers whose stories might have flaws that can be fixed by experts.

The insidious result is that young playwrights often become unsure of how their stories should unfold, and they are not told that the way their sentences unfold might determine the course of their stories. It is a different kind of listening, to listen to how the phrase unfolds as opposed to listening only to how the story unfolds. Surely stories are important—just as having a subject is crucial for the painter. But playwriting will no longer be considered an art form if we are deprived of the paint—that is to say, our language.

14. Investing in the character

The language of "investing in the character" is the language of capitalism. One might go further and say that investing in the character because we have secret information about the character is the language of insider trading (which is immoral even to the most ardent capitalist). Rather than *investing* in characters, might we *feel* something about characters because they too feel? In life, when eyebrows are raised or yawns are yawned, we raise our eyebrows and yawn right back. Emotional identification, neurologists might argue, comes from mirror neurons rather than from "knowing" information. Some might argue the more you know, the more you identify. However, the reverse is sometimes the case; the more one knows about the mysterious lady in the black hat, the less one identifies with her.

I suppose I'm suggesting that the body and mind of the actor do a great deal of work that is beyond information. The phrase *investing in the character* is related in kind to the phrase *tracking the main character's journey.* Tracking a journey makes us into bloodhounds, following protagonist-beasts that have left footsteps for us to follow. And yet adding *information* to help us *track the journey* can often be like trying to sharpen a knife with the wrong tool, making it oddly dull. The journey of an animal tracker, if it is to be dramatic, must involve surprising changes of weather, missed footsteps, wrong turns. Rather than neatly distributed footprints.

In some works of art, what the audience is actually following is not the protagonist's journey but rather the hidden emotional logic of the artist, which the artist covers with all his or her might. Beckett wrote in the margins of his plays "vaguen" so that the author's footprints were covered with snow.

15. The future, storytelling, and secrets

Narrative is an accumulation of knowledge about the future. We begin in the present and end in the present, and in the middle is an accumulation of future possibilities. But is it important to know the end or to not know the end? Are we imitating life when we do not know the future? Or, in another sense, are we imitating life when we do know the future—that we will all die one day? And is it important to imitate life?

How do we know what we know as a story unfolds, and when is knowing overrated? In fairy tales the structure is: we know some things and then we know some more and then the story ends. Conversely, in well-made play structure, we know some things and then we know some more and then we know "the real" hidden secret that happened before the play began. The plot structure of this brand of realism has an important hidden reference point that happened before the play began: the secret happened *not on stage*, which, in a sense, makes it more real. In fairy tales there is no real world that precedes the fiction; there is only a fiction that continually unfolds. One might argue that by creating a reality that precedes the fictional world, we actually make the illusion less real because there is less power in the watching of it.

When the well-made play reveals the family secret from the past in the second act, the secret from the past justifies the drama of the present. I believe, however, that very often the drama of the present moment needs no justification, and therefore no recourse to the past. The secret that began before the play puts the audience in the position of being a detective, excavating the past, rather than experiencing the present. The mystery lies elsewhere. In contemporary drama, when the drama hinges on revelation of plot, the secret acquires both more and less significance than it actually has.

16. On Ovid

I grew up on Shakespeare's romances, in which people become asses, and this brand of theatrical transformation felt normal to me rather than odd. But in the contemporary literary world, things that are "magic" are cordoned off and labeled "magic realism." Apparently, García Márquez himself disdained the term and said that most of what happened in *Love in the Time of Cholera* actually happened in his village. In the Renaissance, playwrights could not get enough of Ovid, the poet of transformation, and Shakespeare almost seems to have slept with Ovid under his pillow.

Paula Vogel, who was my teacher, teaches that there are six plot forms, and Aristotelian form, or the linear arc, is only one of them. Aristotelian form progresses through a logical series of cause and effect. One thing happens, so the next thing happens, so the next thing happens, so the climax happens, and so on. Vogel explains that alternatives to Aristotelian forms include: circular form (see *La*

Ronde), backward form (*Artist Descending a Staircase* or *Betrayal*), repetitive form (*Waiting for Godot*), associative form (see all of Shakespeare's work, in particular his romances), and what Vogel calls synthetic fragment, where two different time periods can coexist (*Angels in America* or *Top Girls*).

I would humbly add a seventh form, Ovidian. In Ovid's *Metamorphoses*, he begins, "Let me begin to tell of forms changed." His emphasis, in terms of story, is on transformation, rather than a scene of conflict or rational cause and effect. Gods become swans, people become trees, people fall in love and die, the supernatural world is permeable. This story structure is reminiscent of fairy tales. Objects have magical properties, people transform, and the natural world is likewise transformative. One thing becomes another thing and then another, and there is no clear moral. If there can be said to be verisimilitude in Ovidian form, it is the sort that imitates dreams or the unconscious.

Perhaps change is all-important in most dramatic forms; in the arc play, change is usually of the moral variety—a lesson learned. But in Ovidian form, the play takes pleasure in change itself, as opposed to pleasure in moral improvement.

We now live in an age where people crave magic and transformation. We need Harry Potter. (One might argue that we need Harry Potter because of political escapism. That is another matter.) Still, I would argue that at the level of the story we crave transformation as much as we crave verisimilitude. Perhaps Ovidian form is not taught at universities as a genuine narrative form because it is very hard to teach the art of transformation. Aristotle lays out his theories in lecture form, easily accessible, whereas Ovid simply flies, and it is difficult to teach the art of flying.

17. Miller and Williams; or, morality and mystery plays

If there are two novelists who divide the world between them (Tolstoy and Dostoyevsky, the fox and the hedgehog), then there might be said to be two American playwrights who divide the world between them (Arthur Miller and Tennessee Williams). I think of Miller and Williams as the architect and the poet: one working in the more objective world of building buildings and seeing whether they stand up, and the other engaged in the more subjective landscape of the soul.

Miller, the architect, builds incredible scaffolds; one climbs them until one reaches the moral: "Attention must be paid." Or: "They were all my sons." His plays build to these cries of the heart, and these cries of the heart sit solidly on top of the scaffold of the plot. Whereas Williams redirects our eye to the moment; every moment is emotionally or aesthetically important for its own sake, rather than having an additive effect. The dialectic between the architect and the poet in modern dramaturgy reminds me of the old dialectic between morality and mystery plays. The morality plays had a clear moral for Everyman; the mystery plays (like the Passion) had an emotional effect harder to cognitively capture. Shaw is in the tradition of the morality plays; Beckett in mystery plays.

One could argue that Kushner's *Angels in America* is the perfect American play because of its seamless equipoise between the morality play and the mystery play. It had a definite moral, one that the nation needed desperately to hear, but also spoke to the metaphysical, irrational world of angels and death. As such, it offered both Miller's moral imperative and Williams's emotionality and brought two disparate strands of American dramaturgy together while creating its own form.

18. Calvino and lightness

Italo Calvino has a wonderful essay, "Lightness," in which he honors lightness as an aesthetic choice and a difficulty, rather than as something to be easily dismissed. You cannot, after all, get something airborne on a mere whim, no—it requires careful patience and some physics to get a plane in the air. When I worked on a translation of *Three Sisters*, I was thrilled to learn that in the original Russian, Olga said quite literally, "I can now remember with some lightness." So often Chekhov is played by actors who are remembering with some heaviness.

A suspicion that lightness is not deeply serious (but instead whimsical) pervades aesthetic discourse. But what if lightness is a philosophical choice to temper reality with strangeness, to temper the intellect with emotion, and to temper emotion with humor. Lightness is then a philosophical victory over heaviness. A reckoning with the humble and the small and the invisible.

19. Satyr plays inside tragedies

In ancient Greece, comedies used to be appetizers in the form of satyr plays performed before the main course—a tragedy. Now we don't have daylong festivals of both comedies and tragedies, so now do satyr plays need to be contained inside tragedies? (That is to say, the dark comedy?) I have never had much patience with separating genres into distinct categories. Maybe that is because I long for the time when we sat all day in the sun and laughed for a while, then wept while masked actors wailed, and both the humor and the desperation of life were illuminated on one day.

20. On knowing

I worry that choosing the essay form implies that I know something. Because today (it is, mind you, an extremely hot day) I feel that I know next to nothing. Recently, I met a mathematician who described himself as "the world's leading expert on absolute and total ignorance." Today, I stand with the mathematician. But the mathematician, while an expert in ignorance, also believed firmly and enthusiastically in the concept of progress.

I'm not sure that I believe in progress, because I make theater. And theater, by its nature, does not believe in progress. We must constantly go back to go forward. And theater cannot believe in absolute knowledge, because usually two or three characters are talking and they usually believe two or three different things, making knowledge a relative proposition. But increasingly in the American theater we are led to believe that plays are about knowing, or putting forward a thesis.

Today, I stand humbly with the mathematician. I am not the world's leading expert on absolute and total ignorance. But the importance of knowing nothing is underrated.

21. The necessary

What seems like the least necessary thing in your play might be the most necessary thing. What seems like the most necessary thing in your play might be the least necessary thing. Maurice Maeterlinck elaborates on this point in his essay "The Tragical in Daily Life": "The only words that count in the play are those that at first seemed useless . . . Side by side with the necessary dialogue will you almost always find another dialogue that seems superfluous; but examine it carefully, and it will be borne home to you that this is the only one that the soul can listen to . . . for here alone is it the soul that is being addressed."

Be suspicious of an expert who tells you to cut a seemingly unnecessary moment out of your play. The soul of your play might reside there, quietly, inconspicuously, glorying in its unnecessariness, shining forth in its lack of necessity to be. The word *expert* was invented after the Renaissance, a time when plays sallied forth in all their beautiful ignorance.

22. Can one stage privacy?

Can one stage privacy, and if one could, would one want to? Is the stage an anti-privacy medium, as opposed to the novel, which is all about interiority? If the novel had its roots in the oral epic, when deeds were sung, and then deeds got written down, and if interiority was only invented in late antiquity, is the theater too ancient a form for the interior? Film has the close-up, but what is theater's equivalent? The monologue dramatizes privacy, and yet, not really, because one is saying one's thoughts aloud to the audience, in open admission that there is an audience.

The stage feels to me like an anti-privacy medium, and yet I like plays that make visible the interior. That is to say, the interior of a person rather than the interior of a living room. As our plays culturally become more and more about the indoors—living rooms, bedrooms, and offices—are they also increasingly about the exteriors of people?

23. On neologisms

Shakespeare invented about seventeen hundred neologisms in his plays. Apparently, making up new words is a sign of genius or schizophrenia. (Writing plays is a deeply schizophrenic act on the best of days, because you are hoping that several voices will talk to you in your head.) It is my contention that a play automatically cannot be naturalistic if it contains a neologism. If the playwright concocts a new word, then the play is no longer holding up a mirror to reality. Instead, the play is creating its own reality through language.

An assignment: write a play with at least three neologisms. At least one must be an insult, one must be an expression of disgust, and one must be an expression of love.

24. Bad poets make good playwrights?

Bad poets can make good playwrights. But it is not an axiom that works in the reverse. That is to say, bad playwrights do not necessarily make good poets. And great poets do not necessarily make great playwrights. (See the case of Edna St. Vincent Millay.) And yet great poets do not necessarily make bad playwrights. (See the case of Shakespeare.) So what is a bad-to-indifferent poet to do? Enroll immediately in playwriting school. Put the bad poetry in the mouths of outlandish characters. It might make the bad poetry funny instead of sad.

25. The place of rhyme in theater and is it banished forever?

The leap Ibsen made from *Peer Gynt* to *Hedda Gabler* represents an enormous cultural leap from the rhymed to the unrhymed—can we ever go back to *Gynt*? Theater is by and large now in the language of prose, rhyme banished to musical theater.

Oh, the memory of rhyme and its populist primordial power . . . Shakespeare's rhymes, his rhymes! Did the rise of the novel coincide with rhyme's banishment from the stage? Why has rhyme become an embarrassment? Homer used rhyme to help remember his poetry. Actors once used rhyme to remember their parts. Do actors have better memories now? Now that they have to memorize prose purposely broken to resemble real speech, whatever that is?

And what of audiences? We remember Shakespeare's great couplets because they are rhymed. It is hard now to leave a play and remember a line because they are all in prose. The meter of poetry used to be thought to have a curative effect: the ancients used certain meters to calm the breast and other meters to inflame. Did we lose some of the medicinal power of language in the theater when we lost meter? Did we abandon the ancient origins of theater as song?

Perhaps we have lost the guiding force of form; we live in the age of prose. Everything is goop. I long for that alchemical thing where the meaning *was* the *sound*—wherein the sound of the word can actually imitate experience. If we trained playwrights' ears rather than their parabolic sensibilities (that is to say, their ability to make an arc), what would our plays look and sound like?

Did the rise of subtext correspond to the rise of prose on stage over and above poetry on stage? Is it possible to use subtext when speaking Molière's couplets or Shakespeare's verse? How to indicate subtext when singing a song from *The Tempest*? One speaks or sings, "Full fathom five thy father lies," and one thinks something different? Impossible.

Part Two

* * * * * * * * * * * * * * * * * * *

On Acting in Plays

26. On nakedness and sight lines

I do not take lightly the burden of putting a naked actor on the stage. I only request nakedness when the subject matter seems to require it. In my play *In the Next Room, or the vibrator play*, the most intimate scene involved not vibrators but a woman undressing her husband and seeing his body for the first time.

When we did the play at the Lyceum Theatre on Broadway, the press asked me constantly about the nakedness. "What's the big deal!" I would say. "But the duration!" they would say. "It's a matter of seconds," I would say. "It's in our face!" they would say. "Really?" I would say. "Do you mean to offend the audience?" they would say. I was bewildered. Why was a sophisticated New York audience making such a big deal out of a little nakedness on stage?

Well, as it happened, the director, Les Waters, and I had been seated house left during all of the previews. On the last preview before the press came, I happened to sit on extreme house right. Sure enough, poor, gallant Michael Cerveris was frontally exposed to the audience for an impressive five minutes. I had late-night phone calls with Michael and with the exquisite Laura Benanti, who played opposite him. Laura: "His penis is upstaging me. They aren't hearing what I'm saying, because they're looking at his penis." Michael: "Unfortunately, my penis is on the same side of my body as my face." Laura: "Precisely. You're upstaging me." (I have invented some of this dialogue to give you the general flavor.)

In any case, I was determined to fix the situation. On our last day of rehearsal, Les Waters was suffering from a migraine and lying down in the dark. I was five months pregnant with twins, full of hormones and possibly a savior complex. I charged to the theater, calling the wonderful Roy Harris, stage manager extraordinaire, a man who has spent a career successfully handling all kinds of desperate people and divas, saying, "Roy, I'm coming to rehearsal. We have to fix the sight-line problem with Michael's penis." "What?" said Roy.

"We've all been sitting on house left," I said, frantic. "House right gets full frontal for five minutes." "No," said Roy, "you're not coming to rehearsal to fix Michael's penis. That's Les's job." "But Les has a migraine." Roy: "It's not your job, Sarah." I, close to tears: "But the press comes tonight and the penis sight lines will never be fixed." Roy: "Sarah, go home. Rest up." "What? Go *home*?" I said, incredulous. "Yes, go home," said Roy, emphatic. I was so mad. "Go *home*?"

And so I went home. And Michael's nakedness was bold and beautiful and unashamed. He did not cheat upstage to appease house right. They had to be reminded of reality in that moment—for nakedness is always real on stage, just as eating on stage is real, and kissing on stage is real, and dogs on stage are real—and one can only bear reality in small doses. In any case, Michael's bravery triumphed over my desire to placate house right so they would better hear my dialogue.

We opened a week later, and I started to bleed, and my doctor told me to go home immediately on bed rest. "Go *home*?" I said, incredulous. "Go home," she said, emphatic. And I did.

27. The four humors: an essay in four parts

Is it possible that modern psychology is closer to the medieval humors than we ever thought? Medieval doctors thought we had four humors or temperaments—choleric, melancholic, sanguine, and phlegmatic. This theory of the emotions held that our feelings proceeded from fluids in the body—yellow bile, black bile, blood, and phlegm. In this theory of the emotions (which Shakespeare inherited from Aristotle), Hamlet would be described as melancholic—full of black bile. The psychological roundedness of characters in the Renaissance was based on the humors rather than on Freudian insights.

Now that we can obtain medication quite easily from our doctors to adjust serotonin levels in our brains, do we still hold with a theory of the emotions that is essentially disembodied and based on secrets? And what are the implications for actors if emotions are bodily experiences to be neurologically replicated, rather than psychological back bends?

The experience of motherhood acquainted me more intimately with the humors and convinced me that emotions are more embodied than I'd ever imagined. To investigate the four humors and their deeply embodied emotional logic, I offer a short memoir of black bile, blood, phlegm, and choler.

On Black Bile

When I was pregnant with twins, around week twenty-five, I started to itch. An intractable itch. No casual itch, this was the itch of Marat in his bathtub, scratching until I bled. The itch started in my hands and feet, in the afternoon, until it spread over my whole body by nightfall. I applied lotion. I put on a humidifier. I scratched. I took Benadryl. I scratched. I rubbed ice on my body. At 2:00 a.m., I would take a cold bath. As soon as I got out of the bath, I itched. I wrapped myself in cold wet towels.

My doctor told me that sometimes pregnant women get itchy, it's normal. That seemed like a banal description of my experience, so I trolled around the Internet, eventually finding a website called itchymoms.com. Here I learned about a condition called cholestasis of the liver, in which bile leaks into your bloodstream, slowly poisoning your bloodstream, causing a terrible itch; and, more important, it can immediately kill the babies.

I went to see my doctor. He assured me I did not have cholestasis of the liver. "It's very rare," he said. "But I have all the symptoms," I said. "How do you know?" he asked. "Itchymoms.com," I said.

Doctors are not terribly interested in the online research of anxious patients, or in websites like itchymoms .com, which had online memorials for stillborn babies, but he said he would do a blood test to reassure me. It took a week for the blood test to come back. In the meantime, I itched. I went to a hypnotist. For a wonderful hour, he convinced me that I did not itch. The hour was up. I itched.

A week later, my test came back, positive for cholestasis of the liver. Now, rather than seeing the tolerant, kindly faces of doctors indulging their anxious patient, I saw the stern and compassionate faces of doctors trying to make life-and-death decisions.

"Every three days," they said, "we will do an ultrasound to make sure there is still fetal movement. We cannot promise that in the intervening days the fetuses will not expire." (I believe at this point they changed their language from "baby" to "fetus.") They made sure I knew that they could make me no promises about the safety of the babies while trying vaguely to reassure me that everything would be all right.

Every four days I would struggle into a taxi with my large belly from my homebound state to advanced maternal-fetal medicine to see if the babies had died inside of me. My great-aunt Laura delivered stillborn twins in Iowa in the 1950s. I worried that it was genetic.

Every four days we did an ultrasound, and my heart would stop until I saw the babies moving. If they were sleeping, the doctors would tap on my belly to wake them up. Baby B moved more than baby A. I could feel baby A's fingers move gently across my belly. Baby B made more global movements. The doctors reminded me if I stopped feeling the babies moving, I should go straight to labor and delivery.

At two days before thirty-six weeks, my bile levels rose. I called the doctor in the middle of the night, sitting on the bathroom floor, wrapped in cold wet sheets, in a circle of hell reserved for pregnant women, fearing that the increased symptoms meant that increased bile in my bloodstream was poisoning the babies.

The doctor said they would do an amniocentesis to see if the babies' lungs were developed enough to justify early delivery. The doctor put a large needle in baby B, my girl. Girls' lungs develop faster than boys'. The test said her lungs weren't ready. The doctors were walking a razor's edge between the mounting danger of carrying the babies in a poisoned bloodstream and delivering them too prematurely. They gave me steroid shots, to help the babies' lungs develop. We waited.

Two days later, my doctor told me to go to the hospital. He said there were no beds in labor and delivery, that I should say I couldn't feel any fetal movement in order to get a bed. Superstitious, I longed not to say those words. But I did say them, to get a bed.

When we got there, the doctor said, "How are we delivering these babies?" "Just take them out," I said. He said, "I'm happy to do a C-section, but baby A is positioned head down and baby B is breech. It's a perfect position for a vaginal delivery, especially since you've already had an almost ten-pound baby." I said, "I think I'm too tired to deliver two babies. I've been on bed rest for three months." He said, "Just push one out. I promise I'll take care of the other one; I'll pull her out by the legs." "Okay, if you say so," I said. I was already starting to look upon this man as my savior, a superhero in scrubs.

I got my epidural. I got my Pitocin drip. We watched basketball on television. At midnight time sped up, and they rushed us to the OR. Everyone in scrubs, just in case. My doctor put on his birthing mix tape. I think it began with "American Woman."

I pushed William out, looking into the face of my husband.

I heard a baby cry. "Is he all right? Is he all right?" "Yes, he's perfect."

Then the doctor reached inside me, as he'd promised, and pulled Hope out by the legs.

"Is she all right?" "Yes, she's perfect."

I began shaking. I delivered the placenta. I shook. My

teeth chattered. They placed both babies on me. I settled. The shaking stopped.

On Blood

And then I bled.

On Phlegm

Then I nursed the babies, one on each side, and then I was paralyzed on one side of my face and thought I had a stroke, but it was only Bell's palsy. The hour we were supposed to leave the hospital with the babies, William was lying in his bassinet and he choked on his own spit-up and his lips turned blue and then they rushed him to the NICU.

On Choler

They put William in a little plastic box and monitored his breathing. They wanted us to leave Hope overnight under a yellow lamp because her face was yellow with jaundice. I didn't want to leave her.

I asked, "Couldn't I stay in the hospital because I got a

paralyzed face?" "No," they said, "your insurance won't cover it."

So we went home without our babies. I remember the silent car ride, looking out the window.

We went home and slept a little. The phone rang. Phone rings are not good when your children are in the NICU. I expected the call to be about William. But Hope had a breathing episode in the night. She was rushed to the NICU.

We ran to the NICU in the ice and cold. Once there, I saw William in his little plastic box, breathing. "Where's my other one?" "You mean baby B?" "Yes, Hope." "She's sicker than your boy, so she's over there." "Sicker than? What does that mean?" "I don't know. You'll have to ask the doctor when he rounds."

A nurse took me to Hope. She was in a little plastic box, attached to monitors. I wanted to take her out, hold her, and feed her. I asked if I could move Hope toward William so I could feed them both. "No," they said. "We don't have enough chairs." I spent a lot of time feeling angry at the nurses, for having dominion over my babies, for not knowing my children's names, and for not having chairs. The more angry I got with the nurses, the more food I brought them so they would remember to keep my babies alive. I brought the nurses donuts so they might hold the babies a little extra in the night, take them out of their plastic boxes, say their names.

Now, as I was writing that sentence in my office, William and Hope ran in.

Hope said, "William, I had a question, did you draw these drawings?"

William said, "Yes."

Anna walked in. "I'm starved," she said. "Can I have something to eat?"

William said, "I'm starved too."

28. Greek masks and Bell's palsy

I was diagnosed with Bell's palsy, a usually temporary paralysis of the face, or the cranial nerve, by a lactation consultant. In the hospital, while I was nursing, she said, "Your eye looks a little droopy," and I said, "Yes, I'm Irish!" She said, "That's not what I mean. Look in the mirror." I looked in the mirror, and the left side of my face had fallen down.

That side of my face didn't move for about a year. I tried to develop odd ways of signaling approval, or friendliness. I vocalized more. I made weird gestures with my hands upon seeing people I liked, as I was unable to smile at them naturally upon recognition. When my babies first smiled at me, I tried to smile back, but I feared the sideways effort looked more like pain.

Eventually, I learned to blink again and I stopped drooling and I could almost whistle and eat spaghetti again (although not at the same time), but I still could not smile.

One day I was watching auditions for my translation of *Three Sisters* and watching all the crying Mashas. Behind these deeply expressive actors was a mirror. I could see myself watching them, expressionless, a mask.

And I wondered, do actors need to experience the sadness in order to express the sadness? Can one experience joy when one cannot express joy on one's face? Does the smile itself create the happiness? Or does happiness create the smile? There was once a neurological study that measured actors' physiological condition after acting. There was no physiological difference between an actor who had experienced grief on stage and a regular person who experienced grief. This made me pity actors.

And what of symmetry and beauty? Botox creates a paralysis that is symmetrical and therefore beautiful; Bell's palsy creates a paralysis that is asymmetrical and therefore unpleasant. A beautiful smile is nothing if not a flash, a revelation, of symmetry. A spontaneous, perhaps slightly aggressive flash of teeth, saying, *I will not eat you. But I like you.* We know that, biologically, symmetry is pleasing; even fruit flies like it.

But where do we put all the asymmetrical people? The asymmetrical stories? Where do we put the crooked people? The people with one leg, lazy eyes, crooked grins? Do we write plays for them? Do we make theaters for them? If symmetry is beauty but life is asymmetrical, then how can art imitate life with an expression of formal beauty that is also true?

I do not know. I do know that an old man walked toward me today and smiled at me. Without thinking, I smiled back. Crooked, but impulsive, and therefore with joy.

29. Greek masks and star casting

When a star is cast in a play, what does the audience see, other than the play? The audience also sees the actor's persona, underneath the language, or above the language, which is, in a way, like watching a masked actor. We are watching, superimposed, the three-dimensional mask of all the old photographs of the actor we have seen before in a *Playbill* or *People* magazine. The actor's face has been made into an individual mask by all the pictures taken of it. And I believe the big difference between the mask of celebrity and the Greek mask is that the Greek mask has to do with the universal, whereas the mask of celebrity has to do with the illusion of being able to know an individual from a distance. When the individual we think we know from a distance is put on stage, we think about all the wrong things. We think about individual neuroses rather than the primal universal.

In effect, one might argue that the relationship between

nobodies and somebodies has now been reversed in the theater. It used to be in Shakespeare's time that nobodies, actors, would play royalty, somebodies. Now there is no royalty in our culture but for actor-celebrities themselves. So now the actors are somebodies in real life while on stage they pretend to be nobodies. And we no longer write about royalty on stage; we write about the common man.

What does that do to mimesis or to the sense that we are seeing something important on stage? When a nobody pretends to be a somebody, the transformation is magical. But when a somebody pretends to be a nobody, are we just watching for a glimmer of the somebody inside the nobody? There is no royalty inside the story anymore, only inside the image.

One might argue that in the age of plastic surgery, Botox has become our new version of the Greek mask. But why would we want immobility in the most facially expressive of all art forms? In order to approximate an ancient mask? The Greek mask is placed *on top* of the face, as opposed to the mask *being* the face, as we have in Hollywood. If the mask *is* the face, as opposed to the face being *below* the mask, then subtext rules the day. That is, when Botox renders the forehead a mute sculpture, we are unable to tell what actors are thinking while they are speaking, and subtext has even more primacy. For a celebrity with a deeply Botoxed face, the purpose of the face is to *not* express. The language speaks, and the face hides. The face hides meaning and expresses beauty. For the Greeks, the ritual mask exposed the voice, which was a very large howl. We do not howl in the movies. And I think it has become bad form to howl in the theater. Because howls are the enemy of subtext.

30. Subtext to the left of the work, not underneath the work

If you're acting in a play of mine, and I say this full of love for you, please, don't think one thing and then say another thing. Think the thing you are saying. Do not think of the language of the play as a cover or deception for your actual true hidden feelings that you've felt compelled to invent for yourself. Don't create a bridge between you and the impulse for the language; erase the boundary between the two. Think of subtext as to the left of the language and not underneath it. There is no deception or ulterior motive or "cover" about the language. There are, instead, pools of silence and the unsayable to the left or to the right or even above the language. The unsayable in an ideal world hovers above the language rather than below. Think of the word *hover* over and above the word *cover*. Perhaps it is because I am from the Midwest, but I think it is almost ontologically impossible to truly think one thing while saying another thing. It creates an acting muddle in the theater and a sociopath in life.

31. On Maria Irene Fornes

Maria Irene Fornes was once my teacher. She objected to the language of intention in the method school of acting, to the constant refrain: "What does my character want in this scene?" One day she said to us, "Who always wants something from someone else? Only criminals. And Americans."

I visited her recently at a nursing home in New York. She now has advanced Alzheimer's. When I saw her, she couldn't speak, and she had no preferences. My friends and I wheeled her to see the birds, then the fish. I thought she might prefer one to the other, but she didn't seem to.

I thought about the will and wanting. I had always agreed with Irene that life and theater are not essentially about wanting something from another person. And then I had children. After which, I would add to Fornes's thesis: Who always wants something from someone else? Only Americans. Criminals. And two-year-olds.

Perhaps what Fornes was advocating was a theater of

desire, transformation, and grace over and above simple want. When I visited Irene, she seemed to have no wants. I hoped that the simple act of being together was enough, as it was for so many of her characters, suspended in a state of communion. She once said to us in class, "American actors are taught to have objectives—what does your character want from the other character? That is *business*. When I deal with other people, I don't *want* something from them; I want a rapport. Some people say that's an objective—it's not—it's a sensation of well-being. Life is not constantly about wanting to get something from somebody else. Life is about pleasure."

I hope, dear Irene, that you are in a sensation of well-being now, whether you are watching the birds, the fish, or the television. When she started losing her memory, she laughed and told me that she wrote on many scraps of paper "write" and taped them to her walls to remind herself. "I even put them on the bathroom walls!" she said, laughing. "Write."

32. What do you want what do you want what do you want

Last night I was up most of the night with my three-year-old son, William, who had asthma. This morning I thought it would be a good idea to take William and his twin sister, Hope, to buy new shoes for the summer. They probably hadn't eaten enough breakfast, and I rushed them to the shoe store anyway. As we were leaving the shoe store, they both started crying.

Hope took off her new shiny shoes and threw them into the street. "Naughty Hope!" I said. They both kept crying. "What's wrong?" I said. "Are you hungry?" I wheeled them into a bodega and said, "Do you want cheese? Do you want Pirate's Booty? Do you want apple juice? Do you want chocolate milk?" They kept crying and throwing things out of the carriage and kicking. "No, no, no!" they cried. "*What do you want?*" I said.

"I want M&M's!" screamed William.

"No, William," I said. "They don't sell M&M's before eleven a.m."

"I want M&M's! I want M&M's!"

Then I said something that I am ashamed of. I believe I said something like, "Fine, I'll get you M&M's if you promise to shut your face. Do you promise?"

"Yes," he said.

I gave him M&M's and he quieted down. But Hope continued to scream, even when William fed her M&M's, one by one, tenderly putting them into her mouth. Her screaming was getting the better of me, and I asked her, "Hope, what do you want? What do you want? What do you want? *What do you want?*" I was like an actor's nightmare of Stanislavsky.

Then she said softly, "I don't like you."

I stopped and listened.

"You don't like me because I yelled?" I asked her.

"Yes!" she said, sobbing.

"Oh, Hope," I said, "I'm sorry. Will you stop crying if I'm my regular self again?"

"Yes," she said, and stopped crying.

William promptly fell asleep, and Hope became her matter-of-fact, happy self again. I thought she wanted me to guess a *thing* she wanted and give that thing to her. In fact she wanted me to stop asking her what she wanted.

When we got home, Hope said, "Will you play with me?"

"Yes," I said. "But how about you eat something first?"

"No," she said. "Play with me first and then I will eat something."

"Okay," I said.

She began to decorate the stage, that is, a small red couch.

She said, "Here is the audience, here is the stage. Ladies and gentlemen, it's the gigu show."

"What is the gigu show?"

"I am a gate," she said. "You open me."

She gave me a plastic yellow key.

"How do I open you?" I asked.

"Here," she said, pointing to her heart. "Turn the key."

I tapped the yellow key on her heart, and she opened her arms, pretending that her arms were a swinging gate.

"Now walk through," she said.

I walked through the gate.

"Now you," she said.

I stood erect, a closed gate. She put the yellow key on my heart and turned.

I opened my arms, a gate, and she walked through.

She was very pleased. And we did this over and over again.

I had underestimated the heart of my little daughter when she was crying. I thought she wanted chocolate milk. She wanted something more, something that didn't cost anything.

She wanted to open my heart; she wanted to walk in.

33. Non-adverbial acting

I admire non-adverbial acting. That is to say, I like the focus to be on nouns rather than being awash in emotional description. It is interesting to me that playwrights don't often write adverbial parentheticals anymore. For example:

SHE (*hoarsely*): Hand me the broom.

Or:

SHE (*jubilantly*): Hand me the broom.

But is acting training still adverbial? And what do I even mean by acting being adverbial? In non-adverbial writing, it's simple: there is an absence of adverbs. In acting, an adverbial acting style proclaims: I have chosen to do this action *this* way; look at how I have chosen to do it! As opposed to: I'm doing a thing. I'm disappearing into the action, the verb or the noun, rather than illustrating it with a wash of interpretive narcissism. The adverb underlines choices, asks: what is the best "-ly" way to perform an action or to say a line?

There is a wonderful game in the Noël Coward play *Hay Fever* called the adverb game. One person leaves the room, and the group decides in secret on an adverb. When the person comes back, he or she asks the group to do activities "in the manner of the word" and eventually guesses the adverb. An example: someone leaves the room, and the group decides on the word *theatrically*. The person comes back in and says, "Harold, wash the dishes in the manner of the word." And Harold washes the dishes theatrically.

I played this game when I was little and perhaps more recently. In some ways this game contains the essence of acting: "Do the action in the manner of the word." But what it leaves out is the practitioner's ability to simply do the thing, focus on the thing, and not on the manner in which the thing is done.

I think of the scene in *A Midsummer Night's Dream* in which Bottom says, "I will aggravate my voice so that I will roar you as *gently* as any sucking dove; I will roar you an 'twere any nightingale . . . We will meet; and there we may rehearse most *obscenely* and *courageously*. Take pains; be perfect: adieu." (The italics are mine.) Here, Shakespeare makes fun of adverbial acting. Bottom's limitless faith in his abilities to roar gently or loudly depending on the theatrical need, to rehearse obscenely and courageously, is that most wonderful and ridiculous of things—the narcissism of the mediocre actor, or the ass.

34. Being in a pure state vs. playing an action

Sometimes theater makers scoff at an actor who can be "in a state" but who cannot "perform an action." I, however, enjoy an actor who can be in a pure state of emotion, with no need of an action to justify the state. It's a kind of ecstasy, a state of being, unqualified, unexplained. Anne Bogart and Ariane Mnouchkine speak of "*l'état*"—the necessity for the actor to begin *in a state* at the beginning of the play, a state that then transforms. Joyce Piven and the high-octane *commedia* actors who started in Chicago as the New Criminals use four extreme states of emotion that transform speedily, one into the other—happiness, sadness, anger, and fear. In that form of *commedia*, the actor needs to be "stated," or in one of these four states, at all times.

But if one is primarily playing subtext, being in a pure state is more challenging. If one is saying one thing and feeling another thing, one is playing a sense of inner contradiction, or tension, or even of subterfuge, which makes a single pure state impossible. Why do we want to watch people playing a sense of inner tension for two hours on stage when there is already enough tension in everyday life?

Is it possible that the rise of the nineteenth-century director (who replaced the actor-manager) corresponded to the rise of subtext because it gave the director an important job, to help the actor find the hidden secret in the text, rather than have the actor merge with the language?

I remember when Maria Dizzia was playing the title role in my play *Eurydice*, she said in a moment of fear during previews, "There are no pillars to hide behind." "Yes!" I said. I think she meant quite literally that there were no pillars in the set, but also there were no pillars in the language. She was in a pure state, and she was terrified. And beautiful in her terror.

35. Speech acts and the imagination

This morning my five-year-old said, "Let's go to the evil tower." "Okay," I said. She stood up and said, "Here we are at the evil tower." "Okay," I said. By speaking the place, she made it so. Five-year-olds understand perfectly this convention, as did Shakespeare. Here we are at the palace. Here we are in the dark, dark woods. By speaking it, we make it so.

In life there are few speech acts. "I do" is one, when we get married. By saying "I do," we make it so. In the world of imaginary things, speech acts are everywhere. One declares the imaginary world into being.

Method acting has the opposite philosophical stance. Saying one thing, the actor assumes that the real truth is buried or hidden underneath the language. Rather than having language bring to life the invisible world, in naturalism the visual lie is attempted scenically, and language is a cover for the invisible world of feelings.

What is easily understood by a five-year-old—that language invents worlds—is assumed by producers to be intellectually ungraspable by an audience of well-educated grown-ups, who, it is thought, need to see spigots and so forth to represent kitchens, because holding up a mirror to nature—or the sink—is thought to be transcendent.

36. Everyone is famous in a parade

I love watching my children watching parades. They seem to love the simple act of some people walking down a street while other people stand still and watch. I think it must be the most basic, simple form of theater. Very little storytelling, and a distinction between the watcher and the watched. No one in the parade is a famous actor, but they are all famous in the moment because they happen to be moving and the other people happen to be standing still.

37. Conflict is drama?

It has always been curious to me that the first rule of improvisation is that you have to agree and the first rule of playwriting is that your characters have to disagree, and I thought why is that. Is it because many bodies improvising need a certain amount of agreement to stay afloat, whereas a solitary playwright needs the texture of dissonance to approximate the group mind?

I think there has never been a more misunderstood phrase than *drama is conflict, conflict is drama*. Instead of thinking of conflict, I like to think of dialectic, a need for opposites that undermine each other. Or, I think about the need for contrast in painting. Paintings don't need large family fights and mudslinging, but they do need contrasts of color and shade. Of course, watching people insulting other people is entertaining, as are arm wrestling, bearbaiting, and the like. But I'm not sure that it's necessary to the *drama*, for drama is also a spectacle, a thing of interest, a thing happening, an event eventing, which is not necessarily a thing fighting. Though fighting can certainly *be* dramatic, it is not a necessary precondition *to* the dramatic.

What if we borrowed from improvisation a proliferation of assent? A form of storytelling that used surprise as a tool rather than bickering.

38. The language of clear steps

When did the language of clear steps become an overriding aesthetic vocabulary for the jugglers, puppet masters, flying machinists, divas, clowns, minstrels, burlesque dancers, bohemians, that is to say, theater artists who are meant to channel the inexplicable? The following phrase is often heard in rehearsal rooms: "I want to make sure that the psychological steps the character is taking on the journey are absolutely clear." But did clear steps ever make for a good story? (See *Hamlet*.) Characters take a step and then a back step and then a leap and then a strange bedeviled jump, and then they fall over. Clear steps seem more appropriate for a manual on how to put together furniture from another country.

Forgive me, I don't drink all that much, but whatever happened to the Dionysian? (See Nietzsche's *Birth of Tragedy*.) Our theater is now almost entirely made up of Apollos. Whatever happened to the irrational—to the notion that brilliant practitioners of an art form have pipe-lines to the irrational, are accused of being madmen by Plato, are almost banished from the city? They do not need to justify every intuition, as though they were being audited. They do not need their pencils to be terribly sharp. If you are one of those people who played school in the summertime (raise your hands, I was one of them), perhaps it would be good to learn a theatrical skill like sword fighting before coming into the theater and inflicting the role of schoolmarm on what used to be the life of the passionate vagabond.

Words like *liminal* and *unpack* should go in essays about theater and get banished from rehearsal rooms. Where are the jugglers? The fire-eaters? Do we all need a master's degree to put up a play? Whatever happened to the garage, to the basement? Someone, send in the clowns. And free us from pedigree. Actors used to be akin to prostitutes in the public mind. Now we are akin to professors.

I do not exempt myself. I went to a university, more than one, I played school in the summertime, and I cannot juggle, Hula-Hoop with flames, belly dance, or even sing in tune. But were I to choose a course of study for future playwrights (and future citizens), it would include juggling.

39. The death of the ensemble

The director and teacher Joyce Piven once asked me, "What can you accomplish without an ensemble?" Then she smiled derisively. "You can put up a *show*," she said. "And that's about it."

Why do we think it's a good idea for everyone to meet each other on the first day of rehearsal and then learn lines for three weeks and do blocking and put up a show? Where did all the ensembles go, and has there ever been a major writer who emerged from a theater culture not associated with an acting ensemble that evolved a style over time? Shakespeare had the King's Men, Chekhov had the Moscow Art Theatre, and we (if we are lucky) have three weeks of rehearsal with an Equity cast pulled from a large group of talented people who happen not to be in a pilot. What to do? Is it enough to work with the same people over time when an artistic director allows you to, when schedules allow, and when the material seems like a good enough fit? Or must we make new ensembles to evolve new ways of making theater for the present moment?

40. The decline of big families and the decline of cast sizes

Did the rise of birth control and smaller families correspond to the diminishment of cast size, and if so, what then? On stage, a small family becomes a symbol of neurosis, whereas a big family becomes a microcosm of the world.

Death of a Salesman has fourteen characters in it. Modern family dramas have four to six characters in them. Arthur Miller was able to write about the relationship of the family to the larger world, whereas modern playwrights are constricted by cast size or their own imaginations and tend to write about smaller families as though there were no world outside the living room.

41. Color-blind casting; or, why are there
so many white people on stage?

If you are a white playwright and you tell a casting agent
that you need a young woman named Mary and ethnicity
is irrelevant, chances are you will see thirty white women,
two black women, and one Asian woman at auditions, and
through some strange, indefinable process, a white woman
gets cast, more often than not.

Chuck Mee once told me that he eventually began to
specify the ethnicities of his characters through the choice
of their names. If you tell a casting agent that you need a
woman in her forties named Aditi, chances are you will see
Indian women in auditions, and you will end up casting
an Indian woman. I believe this has to do with our underlying unspoken faith in mimesis. If the name of a character
suggests a nonwhite person, usually a nonwhite person
will be found for the role. But even if the philosophy of
the playwright is that his or her plays should be cast with-

out regard to race, somehow the structure of theater (or our country) intervenes, and whether from subtle, unconscious racial or mimetic biases, our stages are fairly whitewashed.

I am not interested in writing plays that are specifically about white people. And yet to cast nonwhite people, you often have to specify that a character is a particular race, and then suddenly you have a play about race. Is naturalism, which purports to hold a mirror up to nature, actually just a mirror held up to upper-middle-class Scandinavians?

I remember when the director John Doyle held auditions for my translation of *Three Sisters*, actors would often come in with something I might call "Chekhov voice," a strange accent that is not quite English and not quite American and vaguely upper-class. This unidentifiable accent (which is certainly not Russian) created an odd acting barrier between the actor and the language. John would say, "Where are you from?" And the actor would say, "Detroit." John would say, "Could you do the speech the way you normally talk, the way you talked before you went to acting school?" And then the speech would be liberated from Chekhov voice, and we could hear the language of the play again without getting a brain fog of corsets and samovars.

If Chekhov voice is seen as desirable in acting programs, and if Chekhov voice is an upper-class whitewashing of race, ethnicity, regionalism, and class difference, then what are acting programs erasing? And is the deeply held belief in naturalism in this country an impediment to diversity on stage, in addition to this country's subtle or not-so-subtle racism?

42. *Eurydice* in Germany

The last time I saw a play of mine in another language, it was *Eurydice*, in German. Forget that in German it was pronounced "you'readyke." Forget that they began the play with a prologue by Heiner Müller while people danced in bathing suits. Forget that the father had a very long beard down to the ground that he used as a dancing partner. Forget, for the moment, that there were four flying stones rather than three still stones and that they cut all of Orpheus's monologues and replaced them with German versions of American rock-and-roll songs. Oh, and forget, if you will, that everyone was wearing clown makeup.

The woman playing Eurydice was divine. And I could understand every word she spoke, even though she was speaking German, a language I don't speak. I always knew where she was in the punctuation. And this experience made me wonder: is there an emotional melody or rhythm underlying a play that is beyond translation? And if a very good actor can act this rhythm, then does emotion follow rhythm, and no externally imposed style can intervene? And the experience made me long for meter. Deprived of meter, without the intrinsic rhythm of the Greeks or the Elizabethans, are playwrights now like seamstresses working without needle and thread?

Virginia Woolf once wrote to Vita Sackville-West, "Style is a very simple matter; it is all rhythm." We often obsess in a rehearsal room about what the *style* of the play is. Is it possible that merely by being attentive to the rhythm of the language, even in translation, the actor can attend to the style of the piece, without worrying about stylized gestures?

43. Eating what we see

Recently, I was with my five-year-old daughter at the theater. She whispered and pointed to the stage. "Are those real people?" she asked me. "They're actors," I said.

"But are they real people?" she asked. "Yes," I said. I realized that she must have asked this because of the profusion of digital images that she sees. She didn't wonder if the *characters* were real; she wondered if the *actors* were real. This is perhaps why the new generation will find theater exceedingly exciting (or else exceedingly dull)—a place where the word still conjures images of the invisible world but the people are real.

In the medieval age stained glass was one of the few daily images offered up for reflection and meditation, and now we see God knows how many visual images a day; I think by one recent estimate the eye had to process three thousand visual images a day (and think of Times Square, the horror).

We live in the age of the eye and the hand—one touch, and visual imagery is created, with no word mediating or intervening. We are coming closer and closer to the illusion of being able to eat the image as opposed to contemplating the image. The iPhone makes images feel almost edible. So do food blogs. Simone Weil thought it was important that purveyors of the sacred learn to contemplate the object rather than eat it. Some spiritual training teaches the eye to behold rather than to devour.

Is theater, then, a holding station, a site of resistance, to this feeding frenzy of touch and image consumption? The stage is almost a physical marker preventing us from touching the object of contemplation. Because there are real people acting, we cannot own their image; we cannot *have* them. Perhaps that is why movie stars come back to the stage: to be, without being had.

44. Dogs and children on stage

Recently, my daughter Hope was asking who works. "Do grandmas work? Do grandpas work?" "Sometimes," I said. Then I asked her, "Do little kids work?" "No," she said, "they play." Then she laughed and said, "Do dogs work, Mama?" "No," I said, "dogs don't work."

And it got me thinking about that old adage: never put dogs or children on stage. A dog can't act like a dog; a dog is a dog. Children can't act like children; they are children. And therefore unpredictable. A dog doesn't work; a dog plays.

Is the mimetic function, then, always a form of work? Is that why I find it refreshing to see dogs and horses and small children on stage? Because they are what they are and they are automatically in a state of play rather than in a state of work? (My teacher Joyce Piven has spent a lifetime trying to get both adults and children to be in a state of play on stage.) Why is it so horrible to see certain professionalized child actors on stage? Is it because they are in a state of premature work rather than in a state of play? I recently saw a production of *Annie* and preferred seeing the dog on stage to seeing the children.

45. On fire alarms

When I was working with my friend and collaborator Mark Wing-Davey on *Passion Play*, during our first preview in a church in Brooklyn a fire alarm went off during Act 3. The audience was evacuated, as were all the actors, dressed in biblical clothes on a windy night. On that night in June, one could see a man dressed in a loincloth on the steps of the Lafayette Avenue Presbyterian Church in Brooklyn. After some milling around on the steps of the church, when it was clear we would all be outside for a while, the actors decided to go on with the play.

First, Mary Magdalen began singing a song about a tollbooth, from the scene where we'd stopped in the play. I thought perhaps we'd just have the song as an interlude, but slowly the audience quieted and gathered round, and somehow, one after another, the actors performed their scenes with no blocking, no props, no nothing, in silent agreement. A stage manager improvised a lighting cue with a flashlight, pretending to be a car; a cross was improvised with two actors hoisting up another actor; a sound cue was somehow found on a computer. I kept thinking one of the actors would stop, but in silent agreement they simply kept doing the play. When boat puppets were called for and a wind machine, the actors pretended to be boats and made the sound of the wind. (I thought that once you got your Equity card, you refused on principle to ever make the sound of the wind again . . . but no, these actors made the sound of the wind.) Eventually, we were led back into the church and finished the play, but I longed to stay out on the steps of the church.

I was so moved that telling the story was more important to them than the fear of exposure. I suppose that's always the playwright's hope—that telling the story outweighs the very real fear of total public humiliation. Often there are things for actors to hide behind—costume changes, sound cues, pillars, beautifully painted drops, props, and the like. But on the steps of the Lafayette church, they had nothing but each other, the audience, and the story. And for half an hour, I was as transfixed as I've ever been, remembering that theater is at its roots some very brave people mutually consenting to a make-believe world, with nothing but language to rest on.

Part Three

* * * * * * * * * * * * * * * * * * *

On People Who Watch Plays:

Audiences and Experts

46. On sleeping in the theater

I have enjoyed watching people sleep through my plays. I have enjoyed the sensual fullness of their heads lolling, leaning back, sometimes almost onto my lap. I have wanted to hold their heads as they loll onto my seat, give them a short hair massage. I hope that the play gives them the fullness of a dream. I would like to write a play that purposely puts people to sleep. I would like to import beds into the theater, and couches, and to write a very long play, for a very long nap. If members of the audience woke for a brief second, they would see something extraordinary on stage, like elephants balancing on horses, and they would drift back to sleep, and the dream of the elephant would merge with their more private dreams. And no one would feel guilty, and no one would blame me, because they were meant to fall asleep, a small gift from me to them.

47. Wabi-sabi

I cannot pretend to be an expert in the ancient Japanese aesthetic called Wabi-sabi. In his seminal work *In Praise of Shadows*, Tanizaki praises the hidden, the dark, and the oblique in art and architecture over the bright, the gleaming, the rational. He goes on at length about the pleasures of using a traditional Japanese bathroom, which is dark, quiet, and full of shadows. He defames the Western toilet, with its gleaming white tiles. Are our Western theaters, like our Western toilets, too bright? Too gleaming? Too painted with light?

It often seems to me that our Western theaters, the big ones, in terms of design, do not necessarily resemble brightly lit commodes but *do* resemble airports. (Some of them are currently named after airlines.) Sometimes it seems to me that the whole world is becoming an airport, with more and more glass, with fewer smells to distinguish one place from another, and with nowhere quiet to sit in the dark, or sleep. And yet, of course, the theater is one of the few places left in the bright and noisy world where we sit in the quiet dark together, to be awake.

48. Is one person an audience?

Is one person an audience or is it not an audience? Does being an audience depend on the act of watching a thing, or on watching a thing with others? In a class I taught called Big and Little, devoted to the study of big plays and little plays, we began by writing plays for one audience member. Many students were disconcerted by being an audience of one. When you are an audience of one (in a live theatrical experience, as opposed to a recorded one), you become an actor rather than an audience. No one to laugh or cry along with, you have reciprocity without the possibility of catharsis.

It is wonderful to go to the movies alone. You are with strangers but essentially alone, having a novelistic but highly visual experience. But in a live court performance for one, what is the experience? Part peep show, part therapy session, part forced improvisation on an unsuspecting citizen . . . and yet, part intimacy, part gift.

I determined at the end of seeing many audience-of-one performances that an audience of one was not really an audience but instead a form of intimacy, a form of listening. The audience can be small, but perhaps no smaller than, what? Seven? Ten? In Judaism, a minyan (at least ten people) is required for certain religious rituals. Is there something about ten people that offers spiritual consolation, a sense of groupness, for the neurotransmitters to do the things they do in a group that they do not do alone? To weep from the belly, or to laugh without embarrassment?

49. Chimpanzees and audiences

There was an experiment with chimpanzees and humans recently. Humans were asked to make absolutely no facial expression as they watched chimpanzees. The chimpanzees, without a facial response in their audience, went crazy. And so, when the audience offers no affective response at a play (as often happens), it is well within the actor's DNA to go, as it were, ape-shit. The audience helps to create an aesthetic object through a process of biofeedback. This is why there needs to be a revolution in the concept of subscriber audiences.

50. On pleasure

Lately, I was in rehearsal and I said to the director, "Can I invite my husband and Paula Vogel to rehearsal because they can't come to the performance?" And the director said, "Oh, of course, you must want their feedback at this point in the process." And I said, "Oh no! I had hoped to give them pleasure!" And he laughed with surprise.

Our contemporary theater is at times so feedback mongering that I fear we have lost the pleasure principle. And by extension the notion of reciprocity. Do you remember the old-fashioned notion that artists give audiences pleasure, and so audiences give them money? That notion now feels outdated. There is now the prevailing notion that audiences give artists ideas and feedback and also money—a completely one-way exchange—no wonder playwrights feel so constantly in debt: we are the world's succubi!

I seem to return again and again to the primary roots

of theater in childhood. The child puts on a play for parents or neighbors. The child gives pleasure and in return gets applause. A simple enough equation. How long have we been giving the audience responsibility for helping us to write the play rather than the freedom to enjoy it?

51. Reading aloud

Reading was once something we always did out loud, and to someone. Solitary silent reading came into vogue around the time of Augustine (the 350s), when privacy was invented. Augustine gives an account of Saint Ambrose reading to himself: "His eyes scanned the page and his heart sought out the meaning, but his voice was silent and his tongue was still." It must have seemed terribly antisocial, even for a monk. Now all of our acts of reading and writing are instantly transmittable, in silence. In the digital age, we read and digest texts and silently text back, never having read them out loud.

Theater in its most basic form is a kind of reading aloud. When children are small, we tell them to make a circle and we read to them. When they grow up, we tell them to sit in a corner and read to themselves. In the theater, we ask adults to be children again, to sit in a circle and be read to.

I enjoy the sensation of being read to in a theater as

opposed to watching people behave behind glass. Sometimes, however, because of the aesthetic of a particular production, I feel as though I were watching people from behind a pane of glass.

I have occasionally watched my own plays from the sound booth, where there is a pane of glass between me and the production. When I do this, I am turned into an observer-criminal. Putting glass between the observer and the observed almost seems to imply the possibility of violence.

So to break the fourth wall, or the implied wall of glass, for the actor to read to, speak to, sing to the audience, is an ancient form of communication, which now seems almost revolutionary. Don't make a wall of glass between your play and the people watching. Don't forget they were once children, who enjoyed being read to, or sung to sleep.

52. Buber and the stage

Martin Buber writes in his book *I and Thou*, "I consider a tree. I can look on it as a picture . . . I can classify it in a species and study it as a type . . . It can, however, also come about, if I have both will and grace, that in considering the tree I become bound up in relation to it. The tree is now no longer *It* . . . relation is mutual."

How to give an audience an I/Thou relationship with the stage rather than an I/It relationship with the stage? That is to say, how can the audience exist *in relation* to the stage as opposed to watching the stage as object? Can the play itself encourage an I/Thou relationship? Can a production? We know that a production can transform an I/Thou relationship into an I/It relationship, but perhaps a production cannot transform an I/It text into an I/Thou relation. Or is it up to the audience members and their glorious free will?

If one is to enlist the audience in a mutual relation,

how? Must one live in France to do that? I remember the experience of watching Mnouchkine's company come on stage during an intermission. The children from the play came quite naturally on stage and poured lemonade for the audience (it was a long play). The audience came onto the stage and shared lemonade and bread with the performers and their children, and the stage was no longer an "it"; it had become a "thou."

I'm not sure if this desire to create a "thou" in the theater is shared in the contemporary American climate, where it seems we put all our efforts into becoming more of an "it"—glossy, cinematic, bold. But I do know when I have been swept into a mutual relation at the theater, my knees always tremble from the effort; my knees know something that my brain does not.

53. God as audience: a non-syllogism

If the proper audience for poetry is God, then the proper audience for the novel is people.

Plays have both stories and poetry.

Therefore the proper audience for plays is: people and God.

But: what is the audience for poetry in a godless universe?

The audience for poetry in a godless universe is the academy.

Or perhaps: other poets and therefore God?

And what is the proper audience for plays in a godless universe?

Is there no proper audience for plays in a godless universe?

Must we invent our own gods?

54. Do playwrights love the audience and should they?

During previews in New York, many playwrights develop a strangely hostile relationship with the audience. It is as though the audience were a tactless dinner guest of slight acquaintance who has arrived at 3:00 p.m. for an evening dinner party. The playwright is still drying her hair, still washing the vegetables, there is no toilet paper in any of the bathrooms, children are wailing in their cribs, and we try our best to make polite conversation while we braise a flank of meat. The dinner guest, sensing our confusion and hostility, stakes out a corner in the living room and, having been given no pistachios, appraises the eager-to-please furniture. The relation is one of mutual mistrust. From the playwright/host: I wanted to please you but you came too early and I know you don't like me so I hate you. From the audience/guest: I came early to be supportive and your house is a mess and you're not a good host and I hate you and now I will take my leave of you and blog about you. Immediately.

Is the situation to be reversed, and is it even desirable that we love our audience, or is it better for the art that we occupy positions of mutual mistrust, insofar as art is seduction and mistrust is helpful in the act of seduction?

I am not sure that art is or should be seduction, and I am not sure what can be done given the current economic situation in theater and the fact that we do much of our rehearsing in front of a paying audience well into previews. All I know is that when I am in this situation of mutual mistrust, I think back to my very first beloved audience member. She is Pat Watkins, and she is a retired African-American librarian in Madison, Wisconsin. I met her after an early preview of *Eurydice* at Madison Repertory Theatre, and we talked of Beckett, and then we wrote letters back and forth for years. During previews in New York, if the audience seems hostile, or if I'm too terrified to look, I will picture Pat's face instead. Her face is kind. She came to be pleased, and she came to be challenged. Her letters are in my desk. She came with love.

55. Hungry ghosts, gardens, and doing plays in New York

The ideal audience is either wise or innocent; know-it-alls are not ideal. This can sometimes make New York a tricky place for a new play. Another thing that makes New York tricky is the hungry ghosts. Hungry ghosts in Buddhist thought can never fill themselves up. *Will it extend? Will it move? Will it run forever? Feed me!* says the hungry ghost. And if a play were to run forever, could it properly be called theater anymore? Instead, it would be an ossified, strange thing, dangling halfway between live theater, a parade, and an amusement park ride. Think of the longest-running plays . . . What happens to them? What do they become? Restaurants and plays should not be open for longer than the half-life of a chef. I mistrust restaurants that have been open for fifty years and plays that have been running for fifteen years. Can food stay alive that long? Both restaurants and theaters must offer up living food.

I was talking to a group of theater donors in a city other than New York, and they spoke at length about their gardens. Where not to plant bamboo, and where to plant it. This audience seemed to come to the theater to have fun. I thought, Oh my, they get what they need essentially from their gardens. And they get other pleasures from the theater. Perhaps when we don't have gardens, we come to the theater anxious, vengeful, cranky, with blood on our teeth. In a perfect world the virtues of theater are similar to those of cultivating a garden—something living, something patient, something always growing. Perhaps in cities where people learn these virtues, they come to the theater hoping to nurture the life span of a theatrical company, rather than wanting to devour or eviscerate one show at a time.

56. Advice to dead playwrights from contemporary experts

To Ionesco: "I can't track the rhinoceros's journey."

To Shakespeare: "You should cut that long monologue. I hate direct address. Also 'To be or not to be,' it's confusing and it doesn't advance the story."

To Sophocles: "I don't get enough information about Oedipus's backstory in the first act."

To Shakespeare: "It is too sudden when the lovers fall in love with each other in the forest. Couldn't they get to know each other a little better first?"

What can a living playwright learn from this? Canonical plays are weird. Being dead is the most airtight defense of one's own aesthetic.

57. What of aesthetic hatred, and is it useful?

What is the nature of aesthetic hatred, and is it at all useful? Is it possible that the people who hate my work the most, experience the most bile rising in their throats—are these people in fact my greatest treasures because their experience of the work is the most visceral and profound?

And what of petty, eviscerating theatrical gossip, and is it at all useful? I recently went to see the Dalai Lama speak, and he inveighed against senseless gossip, and I thought, I am doomed. Because my profession requires large doses of senseless gossip. It is how we cast, how we choose our collaborators, and how we relax at parties. But what is the difference between senseless gossip and true dialogue about an object, an object that meant to please but in fact gave no pleasure?

Are we to believe with William Hazlitt that there is a pleasure in hating? Otherwise, why would we go to the theater, knowing that we will hate with as much frequency as we will love? Does so-called senseless gossip advance the art form? Why do we experience anger when a piece of art gives no pleasure, though it was intended to give pleasure? How is it that we feel harmed? People think that in order to save the theater we need more good plays. Perhaps we need more bad plays.

58. More failure and more bad plays

The contemporary theater is afraid of failure. That is one reason why we have a culture of endlessly developing plays rather than doing them.

But failure loosens the mind. Perfection stills the heart.

If perfection were even possible.

Perhaps we would have more sublime plays if we had more tolerance for and interest in imperfect plays. Because perfect plays are not sublime plays. Shakespeare's plays are weird and wonky and oddly shaped and wonderfully imperfect but sublime. They are as untidy-sublime as nature is. Contemporary playwrights are often encouraged to make tidy plays rather than plays with cliffs and torrents.

In Elizabethan times, when they did not program "old" plays, there must have been many new "bad" plays and a certain pleasure taken in their badness. My God, the pleasure in throwing a tomato at a curtain call. Not to be believed! The soft tomato, perhaps slightly rotten, hitting with soft ripeness the ankle of a beautiful boy actor. Perhaps we have lost our pleasure in bad plays. Certainly we have, as a culture, lost no pleasure in watching bad television. It can be equally fun to the average American to watch something considered "bad" on television as something considered "good." (Failure loosens the mind; perfection stills the heart.) Perhaps subscription audiences feel that by subscribing, they have been inoculated against failure. Perhaps theater is just by and large too expensive to tolerate failure. Perhaps we no longer believe in the sublime; we only believe in the tidy.

More failure! More demand for failure! More bad plays! Less perfection! More ugliness! More grace!

59. It's beautiful, but I don't like it

Recently, my son said to me after seeing a ballet on television: "It's beautiful but I don't like it." And I thought, Are many grown-ups capable of such a distinction? *It's beautiful, but I don't like it.* Usually, our grown-up thinking is more along the lines of: I don't like it, so it's not beautiful. What would it mean to separate those two impressions for art making and for art criticism?

60. Is there an objective standard of taste?

No.

61. Why I hate the word *whimsy.* And why
I hate the word *quirky.*

Whimsy was an etymological cousin in 1520 to the word
whim-wham (a decidedly superior word), which had to do
with fluttering the eyelids or letting the eyes wander. It is,
then, a way of making feminine and therefore trivial a whole
school of aesthetic fabulation. We do not tend to call Shakespeare whimsical, although his fairies flew and his witches
chanted. A male artist following his whims is daring, manly,
and original. A woman artist following her whims is wom-
anly, capricious, and trivial; her eyelids flutter, her heart pal-
pitates, her eyes wander, and her hands rise and fall in her lap.

The word *quirky* is so much more loathed than the word
whimsy that it does not bear the time it would require to
dissect its horrors. The choice to have a perceptible aesthetic
at all is often called a quirk. The word *quirky* suggests that
in a homogenized culture, difference has to be immediately
defined, sequestered, and formally quarantined while being
gently patted on the head.

62. A scholarly treatise on the parents of writers

It has been my observation that playwrights' mothers are most often histrionic; the fathers of poets are either brutish or absent; and most fiction writers have very nice parents, but they think said parents are absolutely horrific.

(For evidence of this deeply researched thesis, you can readily look to Tennessee Williams for the histrionic mother, Sylvia Plath for the brutish father, and I cannot reveal my weighty evidence for the fiction writers as it's private information, but I can reveal that they all grew up in pleasant suburbs and their parents are very proud of their work. I know, they send me clippings.)

63. William Hazlitt in an age of digital reproduction

William Hazlitt used to write theater criticism that made you feel as though you were actually there, to experience Bernhardt for that moment only. Now people despair that theater criticism has become (with notable exceptions) more of a thumbs-up, thumbs-down affair. But in the age of mechanical reproduction, when theater is one of the few unreproducible mediums, it becomes even more important for critics to be able to write the kind of criticism that says, *I was there*. A camera cannot capture theater's essence, because its essence is invisible; a pen can. The critic then becomes an indispensable bridge between one century and the next.

64. The strange case of *Cats*

This summer my daughter made me watch the video of the musical *Cats* over and over again. I have heard that *Cats* is a very long-running successful musical. If we are to believe the dictums we read in playwriting books, that one must have a clear protagonist and a clear conflict, what are we to make of the strange, uncanny success of *Cats*? If we were contemporary Aristotles, trying to make generalizations about the nature of drama from contemporary successful works, we would deduce a poetics from *Cats* that eschewed reversal, recognition, and the tragic flaw, in favor of cat makeup, bodysuits, and feline leg warmers. Aristotle made general deductions based on particulars, whereas the particular goodness of every play is particular, rather than a function of its general features. If one surveyed the six most successful plays of the last century, one would have a difficult time generalizing about what features a play ought to have.

Whatever one feels about *Cats* (see essay number 60 about whether there is an objective standard of taste), it derives its power from poetry and spectacle, and from the group mind or chorus on stage, rather than from back-stories or protagonists or inciting incidents. And in so doing, it makes an end run around contemporary drama-turgical principles such as there must be a main character, and that character must want something.

One can imagine T. S. Eliot in the afterlife being pun-ished for his sins, watching a DVD of *Cats* over and over again, projected onto some large cloud. Perhaps he would be moved to revise his dictum that he preferred to give pleasure to the one intelligent person in the audience who understood his intentions and in the afterlife become a man of the people. We cannot say with any certainty. We know only that he would be puzzled by the leg warmers.

65. Can you be avant-garde if you're dead?; or, the strange case of e. e. cummings and Thornton Wilder

How is it that e. e. cummings and Thornton Wilder, who radically challenged form, were transformed by intellectual opinion into treacly sentimentalists for the masses? Is it because they died? Is it because people liked them? When formal newness becomes populist by sheer dint of its ability to communicate broadly in its new form, why is it prosecuted (and found guilty) after death? Will James Joyce's *Ulysses* always and forever be avant-garde because only a certain kind of literary priesthood enjoys it? How to reclaim the dead and enjoyed-by-many and put them back in their proper place as radicals?

66. The American play as audition
for other genres

When American playwrights have had some success in
pleasing audiences, the next logical step is for them to write
for other genres and disappear from the theater (into film,
television, or the musical). When novelists have some success in pleasing audiences, the next logical step is for them
to write another novel. When poets have some success in
writing poems, they go on to write more poems. I have a
fervent wish that audiences would rush the next Pulitzer
Prize winner in drama and say, Madam. Sir. It is our fervent wish that you will write another one of those talking
plays.

67. O'Neill and Picasso

The long trajectories of Picasso and O'Neill were the opposite; Picasso moved from the representational in his early work into the abstract, while O'Neill moved from early abstract experiments (*The Great God Brown*) to the representational at the end of his life (*Long Day's Journey into Night*). Would it be true to say that many long-lived twentieth-century painters moved from the representational to the abstract and that many long-lived twentieth-century playwrights moved from the abstract to the representational? You are already thinking of exceptions—Beckett, Ionesco—who never wrote a family drama toward the ends of their lives, to be published after their deaths. So let me undo the generalization and ask instead: is it anything like the opposite when a painter moves from the representational to the abstract and a playwright moves from the abstract to the representational?

When one is faced with an unanswerable question, it is

perhaps best to digress. I once wanted to be a portrait painter. I wanted to study the face in general and loved faces in particular. I wanted to commit to memory each line on a face, try to reproduce its exact beauty, and keep it. In the end, I was not skillful enough to make a life doing this. And I was suspicious of myself as a painter of pictures, because I was unable to paint *not* from life. The great painters, I felt, could paint from life but also from nothingness. If I'd lived in the nineteenth century, my inability to paint from nothingness would have presented no conundrum. Everything came from life. But now, life is perhaps suspect in painting.

What does it mean for the painter to shrug off life as a model, to see life studies as merely that, studies, preparation for the blazing light of the internal landscape? And what is that model in comparison with a playwright throwing off the solipsism of youth, an inner world of symbols, masks, and the private interior, in favor of a detailed rendering of other characters later in life? Chekhov said that being a doctor made him see the world more objectively. Is objectivity possible in the theater? Did O'Neill's sight become more objective, and do we care?

68. Confessions of a twelve-year-old has-been

I recently came upon a diary I'd written when I was twelve. I wrote in despair, concerned that I had reached my literary peak, that I'd written the best stories I would ever write. This diary, of course, will be summarily destroyed. I am not sure what I thought my literary peak was—possibly my unproduced courtroom drama about landmasses, written in the fourth grade, in which an isthmus spoke. But the point is that even then I seemed concerned about the lack of linear progress in the writing life; that every blank page presented one with the same conundrum, the same terrifying newness, and then, after completion, the downward spiral.

We in America seem to tire of our literary heroes faster than they do in other countries; think of Arthur Miller peddling his plays to England in his twilight years because they weren't produced in the States. Perhaps it is a condition of the twenty-four-hour news cycle in this country, a preternatural hunger for the new. We are still essentially a new country, in relative terms, culturally in our adolescence. We tire of things as soon as we feel we know them. Is that the culture of democracy? A kind of unrelenting aesthetic restlessness?

And so, if one is interested in longevity as a writer in the theater, and also wants to live in this country, how does one respond to the cultural obsession with newness? Or to the sinking and perhaps paranoid feeling that women writers in particular, as soon as they are no longer perceived as potentially seducible daughters but instead as repulsive, dry menopausal mothers in need of lubrication—wait, Virginia Woolf said that Charlotte Brontë wrote badly when she was angry. Let me rephrase. Sometimes it seems to me that the young woman writer is less threatening culturally than the older woman writer because of her newness, her virginity. Her contours are unknown, her language is unknown, she is a mystery. When she grows up . . . What happens when she grows up?

What I mean to ask is: how to have longevity as a writer? How does one preserve one's unknowability in a culture where surfaces are digested immediately and constantly? A culture in which the talk about the art often takes up more time than the experience of the art? Is the answer: to refuse to know oneself? And yet isn't knowing oneself the first principle?

The sense of being a "has-been" is somewhat tautological; one is always a has-been in that one has always

just-been . . . so that if ever one is not in the present moment, then one is perpetually a "has-been," or a "will-be."
Is it better to be a will-be than a has-been? And why is
there no word for being in a state of being, an is-being?
How to cultivate the state of being an is-being? Must
one be a horse led through a fire with blinders on?

69. Is there an ethics of comedy, and is it bad when comedies make people laugh?

Tragedy has a long history of ethical inquiry, but does comedy have its own ethics? That is to say, ancient philosophers have philosophized about what it means to identify with a character in a tragedy and how such an identification refines us morally. In terms of moral identification and cleansing, comedy seems to be more philosophically virginal terrain. Comedy isn't, as we all know, serious. Or is it? I had a dream last night in which I was giving a radio address on the ethics of comedy. What did I say? I cannot remember.

Perhaps serious-minded people dismiss comedies because they are not thought to be as morally instructive as tragedies. But the ethical comedy might teach us to embrace ordinary efforts to overcome folly over and above the tragic impulse, and to laugh at ourselves even as we weep for others.

Still, people sometimes dismiss comedies precisely because of laughter. The laughter was cheap, they say, or of the wrong quality. "It was like a sitcom" is one of the most feared criticisms of a "serious" comedy on Broadway.

My worry is that if plays (in order to be high art) ought not to be too funny, or not funny in a certain way, because it cheapens their aesthetic status, then theater is relegated to the mode of ballet or opera—neither of which is funny, and both of which are historical.

If plays have their roots in vaudeville as much as they have their roots in Passion plays, then their roots are cut off when laughter is viewed as cheap. We theater lovers have lost ground, if television is now the only sacred province of dumb jokes.

70. On writing plays for audiences who do not speak English

I was both troubled and intrigued to be told recently that the majority of ticket buyers to shows on Broadway do not speak English. They are visitors from other countries. I was not troubled that people who do not speak English come to our theater. On the contrary! How wonderful that theater transcends language! But what kind of theater transcends language? And what does this mean for the future of the straight play on Broadway?

It is odd work to be a playwright. You are writing a thing in words that is supposed to transcend words. The language is the icing on the cake. But you are making the cake with words. How is that possible? To make something out of words and ultimately the words don't matter? You are writing language that will not be remembered; most likely, it will be a visual moment that is remembered. You are writing language that eats itself. You are writing for an audience that might not speak your language.

I once began a play with a joke in a language that I thought most of my audience would not understand, in this case, Portuguese. I wanted to see if a joke could be funny in another language. I remember telling this idea to Maria Irene Fornes, and she laughed at me and said, "But that is ridiculous! Jokes are only funny if you understand them!"

Will audiences of many languages but not of the English language take pleasure in plays on Broadway that are preoccupied with the English language? Or is the future of Broadway only in spectacle and song?

71. The age of commentary

Once I went to the Tony Awards. I was breast-feeding twins at the time, so I was distracted by how I would pull my gown down and pump in the bathroom and zip myself back up during the breaks. There were many breaks in the show, and I was struck by what the live audience did while the television audience was watching the commercials. You might think that such a lively teeming mass of gifted performers and producers might be laughing, gossiping, dancing in the aisles, looking over their fans at one another's décolletage. What were these rarefied creatures doing? They were texting. And I thought, The age of experience is truly over; we are entering the age of commentary. Everyone at the event was busy texting everyone else at the event, and a general lack of presence was the consequence. What will constitute the quality of an event in the theater in the future, and how can we hope to enter eventness in the age of commentary?

We are now supposed to have opinions before we have experiences. We are supposed to blog about our likes and dislikes before a piece of art is over.

Will we evolve out of the ability to make art? Will events need to have more violence for audiences to enter them purely, to compete with the gaze of commentary? Or will everything become commentary? Will the country of children be the only country before commentary? Before we can talk? Before we can spell?

72. Writing and waiting

I like to look at people's faces when they are waiting. Do they look bored, rude, thoughtful, do they have a look of forbearance on their faces? The look of forbearance—one sees that look more often on non-American faces, or on faces that have waited in line for bread. Forbearance, cousin of dignity, sister of patience . . . Patience is no longer a virtue in this country, I'm afraid. We've made it into a vice. And I'm worried that the elimination of waiting will make us monstrous. Things we used to wait for: the news, mercury in a thermometer to rise, letters from overseas, boats to come in from whaling expeditions, the fifth act, the fifth course, a turkey to roast in the oven, a pig to roast on a spit, the phone to ring, a tape to rewind, bread to rise, tea to brew, grapes to ferment . . .

And if waiting is lost, then will all the unconscious processes that take place during waiting get lost? And then might we see the death of the unconscious and the death of culture?

Do you remember being a child and waiting, waiting for your father to mix paint at the hardware store, waiting for school to be over, waiting for summer to come, waiting for the curtain to go up, the sweetness of waiting? The waiting of adulthood is perhaps not so sweet . . . the small degradations of waiting, the petty horror of waiting, the real terror of waiting in the "waiting room," the waiting in hospitals, the waiting for death, which perhaps only forbearance prepares us for. Do all world religions mainly teach us about waiting, waiting for deliverance, waiting for the coming of the Lord, waiting for the present moment to pass, because in pure waiting is the diminution of suffering?

Does learning to wait forestall violence? Is plot violence? Is the desire for story and more story a kind of narrative violence? I remember seeing a Robert Wilson piece in which a nail almost went into a hand, over and over very slowly, never getting there, and the violent desire it incited in my breast for the nail to puncture the hand.

Can the theater teach us to wait? To forestall our satisfaction? Poems teach us how to wait. The natural world makes us wait. Erik Satie teaches us how to wait. And so does much music. Will YouTube teach us how to wait? Will YouTube teach us how to die?

73. Theater as a preparation for death

When a beloved person dies, a whole world dies with that person. A world of relation—of not knowing how the beloved will respond. What is left is memory—knowing how the beloved *did* respond. The self must be remade without the relation to the beloved. The world itself must be remade. And so with the theater: every night when a curtain comes down, a world dies. The world of present relation dies, and one mourns the end by applauding.

Perhaps that is why Noh theater makers thought theater was the proper place for ghosts. The basic structure of Noh drama is: a person meets a ghost, dances with a ghost, recognizes the ghost. The ghost leaves. The End. It is difficult for Westerners to see this as deep structure. But from a Buddhist perspective, it is *the* structure. To recognize impermanence, to see the self as an illusion, to grapple with leave-taking—this is one of the structural alternatives to the Crucifixion, to the wound at the center, the scapegoat.

Have you ever seen a Tibetan monk make a butter sculpture? The monks sculpt flowers and temples with colored butter, intricate and lovely, knowing they will melt, knowing that eventually they will feed the sculpture to the monkeys. I think of this on the eve of striking a set, which we do with very little ceremony. We do not have a parade and take the set and float it into the sea, as a Tibetan monk would take a sand mandala to the sea to watch it disappear, and reflect on impermanence.

Many Western traditions pin the arts against mortality; we try to make something that will abide, something made of stone, not butter. And yet theater has at the core of its practice the repetition of transience. We take something intricate and lovely and feed it not to the monkeys, but to each other.

74. Watching my mother die on stage

I first saw my mother die on stage in Flannery O'Connor's *Everything That Rises Must Converge*. I most recently saw her die in *Dolly West's Kitchen*. (My mother is an actress.) When one frequently, as a child, sees one's mother die on stage, one naturally makes a separation between theatricality and reality. The child who sees her mother die on stage prefers to think of theater as make-believe rather than as mimesis.

My mother recently called me because she got the role of the maid in *Hedda Gabler*. She was considering not taking it because it was a small role (I believe she calculated that she'd only be on stage 18 percent of the time), but then she reasoned that at least she started the play and ended it, and at least she would find Hedda dead. I remember when I was a child seeing her react to a dead Juliet on stage when she played the nurse. I was horrified by her grief. A child is not supposed to see the mother in grief; the mother is supposed to die before the child dies.

I remember my grandmother walking into the hospital and seeing my father almost dead, and the sound that came out of her mouth. The sound of age grieving for dead youth, the sound of age not having gone first. The sound came from deep in the belly, and it was almost an animal sound, and it knocked around the clean hospital walls, making the hospital smell less like soap and more like ritual oil. And then my grandmother backed out into the hallway again.

Part Four

* * * * * * * * * * * * * * * * * * *

On Making Plays with Other People:

Designers, Dramaturgs, Directors,

and Children

75. On lice

Lice is the great equalizer. Like death, it comes to everyone. Regardless of hygiene, race, or class, if you have children and they play with other children, eventually they get lice.

In urban centers like New York, nearly every domestic enterprise may be outsourced. Even the eradication of head lice. I combed my daughter's head for two days, proud of my method and dedication, but on the third day, unsuccessful, I gave up and called the lice lady.

The lice ladies of Brooklyn live in Ditmas Park. They are a large family of Orthodox Jews. I find their house comforting. Three babies crawl on the floor, and two men read the Talmud. Extended family comes in and out of the kitchen, here grabbing an apple, there dropping off a child. In the kitchen I plunk down my children to get combed out.

The woman combing is named after Moses's wife, Tzipora. She's twenty-two, has two children, and hopes to have as many as possible. Her mother-in-law has fifteen. I feel that Tzipora and I have a lot in common. Much more in common than most of the mothers I meet on the playground. For Tzipora and I both try to work from home. She combs with incredible patience and pragmatism while her baby cries in the other room. "Schlomo," she yells to her husband, "give the baby a pacifier!" Schlomo is a Talmudic scholar. He also works from home. "I can't find the pacifier!" he shouts.

"Look, I found four baby nits!" she says to me with some pride, showing me the paper towel, then shouts to Schlomo, "Go to the study! He probably dropped the pacifier in there!" Schlomo sighs, leaves the Talmud, and takes the baby into the study to look for the pacifier. Tzipora says, "My husband, he has to study forever, forever." It is now my turn to submit to the treatment. I send the children to look at the fish in the living room aquarium. Tzipora starts combing my hair out. Her combing is gentler than my husband's, and it makes me want to cry to think a stranger would be willing to do this for me (for a hundred dollars). It's almost impossible to comb your own hair for lice when you have long hair. It reminds me that you can't do everything for yourself, that we are in fact primates, that the social contract involves grooming each other. Perhaps that's the metaphysical function of lice. To remind us of our mutual need.

An Irishwoman and her daughter Nora come in for a quick head check. "How do you like Brooklyn?" I ask the pretty brunette. "Sure as hell beats Belfast," she says. Little Nora says, "I like Ireland better," while her head gets checked. They are clear of lice and are thankful. They leave and Tzipora goes back to combing my hair out. "Ooh, I found two adult ones, big ones," she says. "See?" showing me her kill. "Wow," I say. "Thanks."

"So you're a writer," she says, "that's good, you get to work from home?" "Yes," I say. Schlomo yells, "The pacifier's not in the study! You *have to feed him*." Tzipora yells back while combing, "I already fed him at six. *I'm not feeding him again!*" Then, to me, "So you work at home?" "I try to," I say. I realize that the rhythm at Tzipora's house feels familiar to me, the great systole and diastole of work and children, the revelation of finding a sentence in the midst of chaos not unlike the joy of finding a buried nit. My kids come back from the fish tank, claiming they're starving. Tzipora gives each of them a spoonful of peanut butter and sprinkles some baking powder on my head.

And I think, as I'm surrounded by teeming life— parasites, fish, and children—I think, So, you thought you wanted to observe life? Motherhood shakes her head, clenches her fists, and demands, No, you must live it.

76. Mothers on stage

There have been many memorable mothers on stage: Medea, Phaedra, Amanda Wingfield, Mary Tyrone. All of these mothers are told from the points of view of their sons, written by sons. The first is a baby killer, the second a sexually voracious, semi-incestuous harpy, the third a suffocating, self-deluded belle, and the fourth a morphine addict. In short, they are all delightful. Seldom have we seen a mother's point of view on stage.

More recently, we have begun to see a daughter's view of a mother (Marsha Norman's *'night, Mother*, for example). But seldom do we see a mother's view of a daughter. The obvious explanation is that we don't have many playwrights who have also been mothers. The more creepy explanation is that the experience of motherhood is unstageable—beyond narrative and language. Or that the experience is tellable, but no one wants to see it. Mothers aren't meant to have points of view. They are pages, ciphers for their sons and daughters to write their lives on.

But I chafe at this notion that motherhood is unwritable. Some French feminists have asserted that motherhood is unspeakable in our phallocentric language. I prefer to think that motherhood has until now been unspoken about. And that women are as fully in possession of language as men are. For example, Toni Morrison's *Beloved*— an almost untellable story told from the point of view of a mother. *The Joys of Motherhood* by Buchi Emecheta. Sharon Olds's poetry. But I often feel as though theater lags behind the other literary arts in terms of what can be told, because its medium is embodied, subject to all kinds of material concerns that make it slower to change.

The playwright Caryl Churchill is a mother of three; Tina Howe, mother of two; Adrienne Kennedy, mother of two. This comforts me. Certainly many of my playwright friends are reproducing. Perhaps we are in a renaissance of mothers writing. What will the great roles for mothers be? Can motherhood be pressed into dramatic form? Do mothers wish to write about their experience of the little world of children, or when they are not in the little world, do they wish to think and write about other things?

77. On motherhood and stools (the furniture kind)

When I was twenty-six, I directed my own play under a pseudonym. I used whatever limited furniture I had in my own living room for the set, and I purchased a small velvet stool from a junk shop in Providence. I loved this stool because it spun, and on stage it could transform a psychiatrist's office into a barbershop. I kept this stool all these years, and never did I imagine that one day my three-year-old son, William, would also love this stool. Only now, for William, it is a steering wheel. Every morning he goes to the velvet stool and becomes a captain, turning the wheel, sometimes a ship, sometimes a train, other times a rocket. He goes to his stool and says to his twin sister, Hope, "If you want to go to India, say 'Acka Pimo!'" And she screams, "Acka Pimo!" and he turns the wheel, giddy with joy.

I do not know why this stool feels so important to me and why William's game gives me so much pleasure. Perhaps because, often, the demands of motherhood seem divorced from the demands of writing, and I can see both imagination and motherhood in this dilapidated velvet stool. I appear to need to be alone in order to make things; it appears to be necessary to my survival. And yet my children appear to need me, always; it appears to be necessary for their survival. And yet for me to feel my sanity, these two practices, of motherhood and making things, so primary, need to feel as though they are compatriots.

Sometimes I think mothers and fathers need to "come out" as parents in the theater, to make the work of parenting visible in a line of work that has so much in common with parenting in terms of dealing with irrational people much of the day and night and so little in common with parenting in terms of its schedule. But both parenting and theater involve an embrace of impermanence, and both are embodied art forms.

When I had my first daughter, I took her with me to the theater so that I wouldn't feel like a divided self. She took her first steps in a rehearsal room. She came every day with me to rehearsals at Lincoln Center for *The Clean House*, and I breast-fed her in her own little dressing room every two hours. At that time we had just moved to New York and, far from our families, didn't know many babysitters. Unthinking, we brought our daughter, Anna, to a dinner party. Our hostess opened the door and said, "Oh! You brought the baby!" (I suddenly realized that babies might not be invited.) Still, we were made to feel very welcome. We sat down to eat, Tom Stoppard to my left,

John Guare to my right. I was mortified. The baby started crying. I began to feed her. Tom Stoppard raised his glass and said, "A toast, to the only person here who is working!"

When I had twins, I brought them one at a time to rehearsals of *Orlando* when I was still breast-feeding because it was too much to bring both. The costume designer didn't realize I had twins and thought I was dressing my boy in girl's clothes every other day. More and more, it made less practical sense to bring all the children to the theater with me. With my first child, I was able to perpetuate some strange midwestern fantasy that I was a stay-at-home mom while working fairly constantly. Now I had a new reality, a divide that seemed more difficult to bridge.

And so back to this stool, this prop that I love. It is now being used for the state of play by my son, and it reminds me that at times motherhood has everything in common with theater. Both are primary. Both require improvisation. And both require the ability to make junk—garbage, discarded milk cartons, discarded stools—into something joyful.

78. Must one enjoy one's children?

I have a clear memory of my mother saying when I was a child (on the subject of women who worked all the time), "Why bother having children if you don't spend any time with them?"

After I had children, her words haunted me, and often when I leave the house, I have the insistent thought "Why bother having children if you don't spend any time with them?" My mother acted in plays when my sister and I were little and taught English at a Catholic high school to help pay our college tuition. But she didn't work full-time when we were little.

My first conflict between work and children was my determination to go to the closing night of my play *The Clean House* at the Goodman Theatre in Chicago. I was then living in California, and my first daughter, Anna, was only a month old. To assuage my guilt, for the first month of her life, I pumped breast milk in addition to breast-feeding so that I'd have a stockpile and she would be spared the horrors of formula for the thirty-six hours I would be away.

This notion of trying to double up the time you are with your child to make up for when you are away becomes, I think, the strange psychological equivalent of pumping while breast-feeding. Trying to always be there even when you are not. Leaving your milk behind as a proxy for you. Trying to double the effort when you are present to make up for the time you are away. Thinking they will be damaged by any time away from you. And this particular knot seems to be one for the peculiar class demographic of Betty Friedan's *Feminine Mystique*—that is to say, women who have some choice about working or staying home.

Recently, I asked my mom, "Remember how you used to say, 'Why bother having children if you don't spend any time with them?'" She said yes, then went on to say, "I guess I mainly felt, why bother having children if you didn't spend time *enjoying* them." I told her that this phrase haunted me often when I left the house to write or traveled to rehearsals out of town. "Oh, no," she said. "How awful."

I said, "So what did you mean by it? Did you mean that working mothers really shouldn't have bothered to have children?" "Oh, no," she said. "I wouldn't have thought that." "Because you worked?" I asked. "Yes," she said, "but only part-time. I was thinking of the mothers who worked all the time." "So women who work full-time shouldn't have children?" I asked. She took a moment to think, then she said, "Probably I was just jealous of the mothers who worked full-time."

When I was a child, on the nights when my mother went to act in plays, I would hold on to her legs and scream as she went out the door. Then I would happily settle down to stories that my father told me about his childhood. "Tell me a story of when you were little," my sister and I would say. They were some of my favorite nights with my father. But I suppose all my mother heard were the screams as she went out the door.

How many hours spent with children is enough? How much must we enjoy them? How much attention is enough? When I am not paying attention to my children, they appear to desperately need it. When I am giving them my full attention, they seem just as happy to play by themselves. It is as though they need to be certain of my attention in order to play their own games and ignore me. My son has a way, when I'm not looking at him while he's talking, of taking my chin with his hand and turning my face directly toward his. *Give me your full attention*, he says with his hands.

79. The meaning of twins on stage

After I had twins, I got to thinking about the meaning of twins on stage. They are often a plot device: fraternal twins separated at birth and reunited. Identical twins are convenient for mistaken identity, or for the virtuosity of one actor playing two parts.

Often, they are a symbolic device, more curiosity than real people, standing in for surprise, excess, the world upside down when the twins are separated, the world ordered when they are reunited. The coming together of that which belongs together. The hybrid nature of identity. The doubleness of two plots coming together. Undoing the status quo. The Shakespearean image of twins separated in a storm, separated at birth . . . Does the image reflect the primordial feeling that we have been separated from our other, true self at birth, or during another great storm in our lives?

Shakespeare himself had real twins. One assumes, then, that he wasn't interested in twins as a purely literary conceit. After he had the twins, there were apparently seven years, called the Lost Years, in which he did not write. One cannot imagine him changing diapers in Stratford-Upon-Avon—what, then, was he doing?

At any rate, now that I have real twins, I find that I am leery of twin-as-symbol. My twins were a great surprise to me. They bowled me over with the strange audacity and unpredictability of the natural world. (Perhaps in the future twins will come instead to signify the strange audacity and controlled nature of the medical world, now that twins are becoming more common with IVF.) But my twins were a surprise (perhaps genetically bequeathed to me by my great-aunt Laura, whose twins were stillborn). My pregnancy was difficult and Victorian. I went on bed rest for three months. My friends brought me books to read, and for some reason I kept finding casual mentions of a dead twin. *Little Dorrit.* Dead twin. Out it went. I was terrified. Why were there so many literary dead twins? In the Elizabethan era or the nineteenth century, I'm sure it was a fact of life. But on the symbolic level, why all the dead twins? Because two was an impossibility, symbolically? Or because it was a symbol of double loss? We come into the world alone, and we die alone. Not so for twins.

Their doubleness is overwhelming but also their lack of sequence, that is to say, their constant simultaneity. On a daily basis, for the parent, the eye never rests. The eye is always on two stories, unfolding at once. Two protagonists. One child climbs a chair; one reaches for an electrical outlet. One invents a new word while the other is inventing a new gesture. You cannot watch one story unfolding, then another. You cannot fall in love with one protagonist, and then another. You must fall in love with two protagonists at once. The eye looks everywhere at once, the stories unfold at once, and the heart must expand doubly.

After I gave birth to my twins, the nurse laid them on the gurney and they held hands. Before I held them, they held each other. Together, they are something larger, and different somehow from mere siblings. And yet I resist thinking of them as part of a whole. I dislike the word *multiple*. How can a person be a multiple, a multiple of what?

Every day I insist upon this: to love two as one and one. Not to be terribly interested in their doubleness as curiosity or symbol, but to be interested in their particular and individual natures. Perhaps having children makes one increasingly distrust the symbolic world. Because suddenly nothing is as important as the very real particular.

80. Is playwriting teachable?: the example of Paula Vogel

People often ask me if I think playwriting is teachable. Making a soufflé, tap dancing, changing a tire, and making stained glass are all teachable activities, and making a play is not so different from making a soufflé, tap dancing, changing a tire, and making stained glass all at the same time, but on paper. Why, then, do many see the writing of plays as such a mysterious, unteachable activity? Is it because our culture has such a high regard for individualism that it has such a low regard for teachers? Almost everything in the culture is taught, one way or another, but for originality, which cannot be taught and is therefore judged to have the most value. And yet in most art forms, the originality of the individual is assumed, whereas the form transmitted through history is taught and teachable. For example: this is middle C. This is how to point your toes. This is how to sharpen your pencil (which I don't take lightly; I remember when a drawing teacher actually showed me how to sharpen my pencil properly when I was twenty and it made all the difference). But is *playwriting* teachable?

Rather than trying to answer the question in an abstract way, I'd like to tell a story. Paula Vogel begins *How I Learned to Drive*, "Sometimes, in order to teach a lesson, you have to tell a story." And so. I met Paula Vogel at Brown University. I was twenty. I had just taken a leave of absence after my father's death. I was very close to him, and he'd died of cancer, in Chicago, that summer. The first two years of college had been a blur, spent mainly studying and racing back to Chicago on a plane at the first opportunity to see my father. He was diagnosed with advanced metastatic cancer during Thanksgiving of my freshman year. I thought about transferring to a school in Chicago, but my father would have none of it. He wanted everything to be as "normal" as possible and didn't want me to live at home among bedpans. Of course nothing was normal, but I tried to be as normal a nineteen-year-old as I knew how, while thinking of death and illness much of the time. Perhaps my father knew somehow that I couldn't leave Providence before I'd met Paula Vogel, or my future husband.

At any rate, I took a semester off after my father died and spent it at home in Chicago, teaching special education classes by day. At night, my mother and sister and I shared the same house, each in a private house of grief that could not be shared. I came back to Providence that spring and was having trouble concentrating on my studies. It was hard for me to read and hard for me to write. I lived in a blue house on Hope Street. It seemed dark much of the time; the light itself seemed darker, though the seasons were as they always had been in Providence—in winter a damp cold that gets inside the bones, and in spring all flowering trees. Regardless of the trees, it looked dark to me. And then I met Paula Vogel.

What strikes me most when I remember Paula's teaching is her *presence* as much as the content of her teachings. I think in this country we have an obsession with content and curriculum, all the while devaluing presence and proximity, which are teaching values hard to describe or quantify (or, indeed, teach). Paula has a tremendous gaze, a tremendous listening power, and the most intelligent curiosity of anyone I have ever met. She took me seriously.

And so when I was in her class and told her that I was having trouble writing about the things that mattered most to me, Paula said, "If someone asked me to write a play about my brother Carl, who died of AIDS, I'd never have gotten out of bed. Instead, I wrote about a kindergarten teacher taking a trip through Europe, which became *The Baltimore Waltz*. And I was able to write about my brother." Then I remember her looking at me with that uncanny penetrating gaze she has, the gaze of a brilliant scientist making a diagnosis, but with a nonscientific, laser-like empathy, and she said, "Write a play in which a dog is the protagonist." "Okay," I said. And I did. That was a play called *Dog Play*, and it was the first thing I was able to write after my father died. It viewed his illness and death through the eyes of the family dog.

I found in Paula's approach to playwriting a great deal of pleasure and a great deal of play. It was almost too pleasurable, too decadent. I always thought I'd be a poet, which gave me a solitary, ascetic kind of pleasure, not the kind that makes you laugh out loud or stay up late into the night with others. And so I thought playwriting was a wonderful diversion.

I went to study in England for a year and came back a little more mended. I wanted to write a senior thesis on "representations of the actress in the Victorian novel," and I asked Paula to be my thesis adviser. Paula said, "No, I cannot advise that thesis. But if you write a play, I will advise your thesis." I felt a strangled joy in my chest. I told Paula that I did have an idea for a play. "What is it?" she asked with a characteristic gleam in her eye. I stammered, "This town is playing the Passion play year after year, but the guy who always has to play Pontius Pilate wants to play the role of Jesus, played by his cousin?" I remember that time slowed down as Paula looked at me in her uncanny way and said, "I think you should write that play."

And so I did write that play, under her guidance. It took me twelve years to finish, and it was called *Passion Play*. Knowing that I began my writing life as a rather retiring poet, Paula treated me with tenderness and guile, sneaking my play into the New Plays Festival at Trinity Repertory Company in Providence. (This is one of Paula's chosen teaching methods, which she fully admits. She attempts to make students addicted to the dust backstage, that barely there stuff you have to inhale.)

The night of the opening, my mother flew into town from Chicago to see the play. We were driving down the hill toward Trinity Repertory Company when we were blindsided, hit by a car going very fast on Hope Street. I wasn't wearing a seat belt in the backseat and I hit my head and blacked out. Before I blacked out, I remember thinking, This is how death comes, quickly.

I woke up, and my mother thought maybe we should go to the hospital for an MRI, and I said, "Are you kidding? Let's go to my play. We're almost late." So we went to my play, and I remember feeling an out-of-body sense of rapture seeing the play in three dimensions. I knew then that I would spend my life doing this and not look back. (I got an MRI the following day. It was normal. It did not register the change of vocation.)

When I reflect on all the things Paula taught me—among them, Aristotelian form, non-Aristotelian form, bravery, stick-to-itiveness, how to write a play in forty-eight hours, how to write stage directions that are both impossible to stage and possible to stage—the greatest of these is love. Love for the art form, love for fellow writers, and love for the world.

When I got married, Paula and her wife, the eminent biologist and feminist theorist Anne Fausto-Sterling, got frocked for the day. My husband was a student of Anne's.

It seemed fitting that our teachers, who were both so transformative for each of us, would bind us in front of a community.

After we were married, and as I had my first forays into the professional world, it was always Paula I would call first with personal and theater-related dilemmas. She was one of the first people I called, slightly panicked, when I found out I was pregnant with twins. "Come to Cape Cod for a week," Paula said. "We'll take care of you." On Cape Cod, Paula entertained my big girl, Anna, by making Kleenex into puppets. Anne grilled fish. We swam in ponds. This was the house that Paula had taken me and two other graduate students to years earlier. She had told us to go out on the deck, look at the view of the Atlantic Ocean, and say to ourselves, This is what playwriting can buy.

Now, pregnant with twins and terrified for my writing life, I sat and looked out at the same blue. Anne is a great naturalist and bird-watcher, and a great many birds flew over. In a quiet moment I asked Paula, "Will I ever write again?" She gave me her penetrating gaze, almost a form of hypnosis, a summoning. If I were a soldier, Paula would be a general, coaxing me into battle. She said, "Of course you will."

We named our twins Hope and William. Hope Street and Williams Street was the intersection in Providence where my husband and I met. And where we grew up. And that is most of my story.

So, back to the abstract question: is playwriting teachable? Of course it's not teachable. And of course it is teachable. It is as teachable as any other art form, in which we are dependent on a shared history and on our teachers for a sense of form, inspiration, and example; but we are dependent on ourselves alone for our subject matter, our private discipline, our wild fancies, our dreams. The question of whether playwriting is teachable begets other questions, like: is devotion teachable? Is listening teachable? Is a love of art and a willingness to give your life over to art teachable? I believe that these things are teachable mostly by *example*, and in great silences. There is the wondrous noise of the classroom, the content, the liveliness of the teachings themselves, the exchange of knowledge, and then there is the great silence of relation. Of watching how great people live. And of their silently communicating, "You too, with your midwestern reticence, can go out into the great world and write. And when we fail, we'll have some bourbon, and we'll laugh." Teaching is unbounded by the classroom. Just as love is unbounded by time.

81. Bad plays and original sin

According to one pervasive philosophy governing some theaters and new play development models today, the new play is born bad. According to this model, the artistic director is something of a pope, mediating one's relationship with God (which is, of course, the audience), and the playwright is a sinner.

One goes to confession (one's meeting with the artistic director or literary manager after the first reading or first preview) and confesses about how bad one's play is and how one will try to fix it. One can only hope one doesn't get excommunicated if one likes one's own play (or one's own bastard issue) and refuses to "fix" it. In this model dramaturgs become nuns because they are virginal (they're not required to write or direct plays), they are often powerless in a hierarchical institution, they're often very badly paid, underappreciated, smart women, and they rap your knuckles with rulers, it's true, I've seen it in the bathroom. (Not really. Not all theaters or dramaturgs are like this, I should say, nor are all priests and nuns—let me here and now exempt Sister Mary Angelita from Davenport, Iowa, who rigged my mom into her flying harness as Peter Pan.)

But to continue with this tiresome metaphor . . . One's penances are one's rewrites. One grips one's rosary and one's pencil and hopes for the best. The more rewrites one does, the more perfect and clean is the play in the eyes of the church.

In this model of development, the play is born bad. It exists to be reformed and bettered by the church (the institutional theater). The play is also unclean because it is a bastard child, since it is the issue of a single parent and the imagination, which has no flesh. It needs another parent, the church, to become clean. Baptism will hopefully come from a good review, without which the play is also unclean and destined for Limbo.

Now, if you think this is an anti-Catholic rant, you are mistaken. I only think that original sin is not a good model of new play development. Even if it might be a good model for moral development. Look at me, I'm a picture of mental health. Having been raised Catholic and become a playwright in modern times.

82. A love note to dramaturgs

Dramaturgs are beleaguered. They are bashed, silenced; they are badly paid. And still, they persevere. They are bashed by the very people they have sacrificed their own family lives to defend! Playwrights! Already in these pages I've called them nuns. I've accused them of sharpening pencils too sharply. Let me honor you, dramaturgs. Let me shower you with love. Playwrights need you. Desperately. We need you to sit next to us at the first rehearsal when we feel as if we were being flayed open and exposed. We need you to sit next to us at the first dress rehearsal and tell us that it's worth saving, even though we feel worthless and doomed. We need you to sit next to us during the first preview and give us two or three notes that are easily accomplished when we want to leave the theater forever and take up marine biology or nursing or any profession that doesn't involve public humiliation. We need you to be nice to us when the director, or artistic director, or the audience is being mean to us. We need you to deflect strange questions during audience talk-backs and remind audience members that they are most helpful when they describe their own experience rather than trying to fix the play. Or perhaps we need you to excuse playwrights from coming to talk-backs; dramaturgs are better able to answer questions at talk-backs and then gently relate the audience response to the playwright, who might be hiding upstate or incapacitated in the nearest bathroom. We need you to be publicly articulate about our plays when we feel dumb about them so we can do the more private, blunted, and blind task of writing. We need you to be as articulate about unconventional structure as you are about conventional structure. We need you to fight the mania for clarity and help create a mania for beauty instead. We need you to ask: is the play *too* clear? Is it predictable? Is this play big enough? Is it about something that matters? Conversely, is this play small enough? And if the play's subject matter is the size of a button, is it written with enough love and formal precision that the button *matters*? We need you to remind audiences that plays are irreducible in meaning, the way that poetry is. To remind audiences that theater is an emotional, bodily, and irreducible experience. We need you to fight for plays at the theater where you work and in the broader culture. We need you to ask us hard questions. We need you to remind us of our own integrity. We need you to remind us to make hard cuts and not fall in love with our own language when our plays are too long. We need you to drink with us if we are drinkers after a horrible first preview and not drink with us if we are abstainers. You might also train as an actor, or a director, or a set designer, because we need you to understand each element fully. We occasionally need you to leave the profession and become critics, because you truly love the theater, have critical and insightful minds, and would write about new plays with love and understanding. I love you, dramaturgs. The very best of you are midwives, therapists, magicians, mothers, rabbinical scholars, Socratic interlocutors, comrades-in-arms, comedians, and friends. I wish there were a better name for what you do than *dramaturg*.

83. Children as dramaturgs

One problem with the word *dramaturg*: it is so terribly serious and so terribly German, and theater is not always terribly serious or terribly German. Sometimes I think children make good dramaturgs because they are not terribly serious and their boredom mechanism is finely tuned. That is to say, they are bored by plays that aren't theatrical, and we know they are bored because they scream. (Adult audiences use the subterfuge of coughing or looking at their programs when they are bored.) But children can't read, so they scream. I do believe that young children can tolerate a lot of language on stage if there are theatrical moments— for example, if someone flies or rides in on a bicycle or if there are large puppets. Bringing children to rehearsals can tell you quickly whether or not the play is theatrical.

I brought my six-year-old daughter, Anna, to my rehearsals of *Melancholy Play* (in which a woman turns into an almond). I wanted to see if she got bored. "Oh no," she said. "It's the best show I've seen in years."

Then she said, "Your plays balance on air I mean they are air I mean they are performed in air so they are air.

"If a whole city could balance on a seed then a city could balance on a play because a play is air and everything is air.

"Your next play should be about a seed because a seed is smaller than an almond. Or maybe your next play should be smaller than an almond, about nothing, about air."

84. Democracy and writing a play

Making a piece of theater is a democratic act. Writing a piece of theater is not a democratic act. The development process has confused this issue. Making and rehearsing a new play means that every voice counts; it is a collaborative process. Writing a play means that the author is often collaborating with invisible or dead people. When the writing process becomes months of developmental workshops, the play becomes more like something Congress would turn out—baffling, cognitive, and legalistic.

Writers should be even lonelier when they are meant to be lonely (when they are writing), and they should be more surrounded when they are meant to be surrounded (when the play is ready for production). This is the natural rhythm of those odd creatures, playwrights, those misanthropes who love people; who desperately want to be alone and then, two weeks later, when they have finished a play, desperately want to be with other people. The development process has turned everything into a strange hybrid where writers are always collaborating, always surrounded, but never produced.

I have noticed lately that young playwrights often speak of the development process in the passive voice: "I was developed at X theater." Or, "I would like my play to be developed at Y theater." I think both language and practice would be improved by saying, "I would like to work on my play at X theater." Or, "I rewrote my play at Y." For development is really nothing more and nothing less than playwrights doing something fairly old-fashioned—their rewrites. Perhaps there could be less democracy in the imagination, and more democracy in the room.

85. What about all that office space?

I was a founding member of a theater called 13P, which stood for 13 Playwrights, and we wanted to do thirteen plays by thirteen playwrights and then implode. Which we did. The artistic director of every production was the playwright, and there were no offices, and we didn't have a theater, and all our meetings were held at a coffee shop in Brooklyn before we all ran off to our regular jobs. When I did my play with 13P, I was heartened by how a theater could be run virtually out of a coffee shop. We did not require an office for the literary manager, or a costume shop, or an office for the marketing director. And yet most institutional theaters have a great deal of office space.

All of this office space and what does it do at night? When the lights go down in the offices and up in the theaters, I imagine these offices blinking and gaping in the great cityscape, awash with sadness at their own wasted potential. The emptiness! With real estate at such a premium, especially in New York, should homeless actors and writers be sleeping at theater offices at night? Perhaps they should!

These days, audiences have homes and the artists do not. That is to say, audiences and patrons have seats named for them, but actors, writers, directors, and designers generally do not. Marketing people have jobs and health insurance and chairs, but artists generally don't. A couple of exceptions to this rule: the Goodman Theatre has a dedicated room for the writer called the August Wilson Room, with a large desk. Arena Stage and the Public Theater are now giving health insurance to writers and making office space available for them. Playwrights Horizons has a writer in residence, Dan LeFranc. But generally, as ensemble theater disappears and theater artists become more nomadic, institutions become more still, more corporate, more steady.

How can we redress the imbalance of artists having no seats? Should artists not have seats, because the job of the artist is and always has been primordially nomadic and non-bureaucratic? Or should we make the offices work for us at night? Put site-specific plays in offices. Have health insurance for artists. Have chairs and desks and Murphy beds for wayward writers to sleep in at night.

86. Ceilings on stage

Lately I have noticed a trend in theater design to put ceilings on stage. That is to say, to put ceilings on sets, completing the frame in the set of a living room, for example. Does having ceilings on our stages make us feel that we are having a more filmic, or a more real, experience on stage? I have often enjoyed these fake ceilings, though I take pity on the lighting designers (there's nowhere to hang the lights). But I am also suspicious of ceilings on stage.

Theater used to be outdoors and had outdoor subject matter—forests, battlefields, castle exteriors. Then we moved indoors and showed indoor subject matter. But the continued lack of a ceiling in the theater created, I might argue, a primordial connection with what used to be the sky; light poured in, and one understood that a room wasn't really a room, but had a connection to some ancient playing space, by some ancient rocks.

In film, it's almost impossible to imagine an interior

with no ceiling. It would be surreal. Imagine a living room on film with an open sky above it. The meaning that gets made is that the living room is actually out of doors. Whereas a living room on stage constructed without a ceiling is not surreal; it is an accepted mode of not finishing the image, of understanding that theater has an automatic traffic with metaphor.

And so I wonder if by putting ceilings on our stages we are trying to compete with film in a way that will make us automatically fail, making our stages smaller, and making our connection with the sky historical.

87. Storms on stage

In the old plays there were storms. *Lear. The Tempest. Iphigenia.* Perhaps we don't have storms in our plays so much anymore because our plays don't take place out of doors so much anymore. But I think we also don't have many storms in our plays because of a larger dramaturgical preoccupation with characters learning lessons that make emotions rational. And a sudden wind defies this smooth, cognitive version of emotion. A sudden wind is event rather than lesson.

On one hand, a sudden storm in a play is entirely naturalistic—unexpected storms happen all the time in life (more and more lately). And yet somehow the use of storms on stage became symbolic rather than a mirror of nature when theater moved indoors. Why?

Perhaps because storms defy explanation, and emotions in naturalism are explicable, the irrational is relegated to the world of the symbolic rather than the mimetic, though life certainly seems irrational much of the time.

The Greeks seemed correct when they assigned the natural world the irrational personas of the gods. In the wake of a tsunami, what is reason?

In the wake of a tsunami, what has happened?

Water.

Why has it happened?

Water.

What of justice?

Water.

Why anything?

Because water.

88. Snow on stage

Snow is the only thing that comes down from the heavens and stays awhile.

On stage, the verticality of snow reminds me of a kind of grace that is temporary but has some staying power, like theater itself. In life snow can melt, but in theater it is swept away by stagehands. In either case, it is impermanent.

In *Three Sisters*, Tuzenbach says, "Look, it's snowing out. What is the meaning of snow?"

I think he means that snow simply is. Snow reminds us of is-ness. In meaning nothing much, it means everything. On stage, snow reminds us of verticality and of the fact that light things can fall slowly. Snow falls slowly rather than falling with a thump, and so snow is *with* gravity and also against it. Snow appears to slow gravity, so that we can see falling happen.

If rain on stage might be said to be God's tears cleaning away human dirt, misery, and memory, then what is snow on stage? A revelation that dirt can be covered by something clean from the sky? A revelation that cold does not last? That warmth does not last? That in order to make snow on stage, human hands have to stuff paper in a little box and shake it down, pretending to be God in black pants?

89. Gobos, crickets, and false exits: three hobgoblins of false mimesis

Why do gobos,* the sound of crickets on stage, and false exits on stage make me sad? I think it's because they are borrowed from the memory of other mimetic plays. If the world might well be an illusion (as the Buddhists say), then theater is definitely an illusion. And if theater is definitely an illusion, how sad to record real crickets so that they sound like fake crickets pretending to be real. If one's goal is to reveal what we think of as the world to be an illusion, then false exits and crickets won't serve.

What would have happened to the history of drama if Meyerhold, the highly visual director, had been the accepted interpreter of Chekhov rather than Stanislavsky? Chekhov, irritated by Stanislavsky's unnecessary sound cues,

---

*For those who haven't lived through tech week, gobos are lighting tools that create shapes on stage such as the look of a real cathedral window.

once said, "I shall write a new play, and it will begin with a character saying, how wonderfully quiet it is! There are no birds to be heard, no dogs, no cuckoos, no owls, no nightingales, no clocks, no harness bells, and not a single cricket." If the sound of crickets makes us feel that the night is more real on stage, it is more real with reference to a real night elsewhere, somewhere else recorded, someone else's memory of a cricket-drenched childhood, someone else's shorthand for night.

90. Oh the proscenium and oh the curtain

When I work at a theater with a grand proscenium or a grand curtain and walk backstage during intermission, the whole enterprise reminds me of Plato's cave. I am aware of the grandness of the arch and the seeming impermeability between the watcher and the watched, yet all that is required to burst through the illusion is to slip behind a curtain and use the facilities. Slipping through so easily from one state to the other calls to mind the seeming impermeability between different states of being and how quickly they are punctured: between the sick and the well, between the state of being alive and being, well, dead—where the divide seems absolute but the crossing is as swift and simple as passing behind a curtain.

Perhaps that's why I find it inexplicably moving to walk backstage while the audience is still in the house, talking (perhaps wildly and nobly excoriating my play) and buying candy. It is often the back of the tapestry that turns out to be more beautiful than the front: being able to see all that work—the waiting, the drudgery, the pricks of blood . . .

Some might charge that the proscenium creates a less communal approach to theater because of the separation between the watcher and the watched. This is perhaps true. On the other hand, the proscenium is an attempt to replicate the shadows on the wall of Plato's cave and then make the illusion disappear at the end. For the purpose of creating a Platonic illusion and then laying the illusion bare, prosceniums and curtains are serviceable. If a world without curtains is a world without illusions, then perhaps we should hold on to the curtains.

91. Exits and entrances and oh the door

Exits and entrances are important and always have been. "Exeunt," they once wrote. Lately I have noticed that when my four-year-old plays, she madly opens and closes doors. The entrances and exits in a four-year-old's play are actually more important than scenes of conflict. A person enters, and the scene is transformed. A witch enters, a witch exits. A sailor enters, a duck exits. End of play.

One effect of film on theater is that theatrical exits and entrances diminished. An exit has little power in cinema because the camera cuts away before a person actually closes the door. In film, a character's entrance is often edited away. The camera *becomes* the door. In the theater we have doors rather than cameras. They are both openings and closings, cameras and doors. But in the theater, a live person is in charge, whereas in film, the machine, and an editor after the fact, are in charge.

In our desperate and unconscious desire to be more like

film, we contemporary dramatists often end our scenes as though we were cameras. And it can be sad to end a scene as though a camera were cutting away when what really has to be cut away is an entire set. It lacks magic. And it makes me rethink the magical possibilities of the door.

Oh the door! Made of simple wood, standing wobbly on a fake frame, it opens, it shuts, it slams or is quiet, people, things, or animals come out and come in, a person comes out, an ostrich comes back in, oh the door!

92. *Theatrical* as a dirty word for architects

I was recently having tea with my only architect friend who loves Maurice Maeterlinck, and he mentioned that the word *theatrical* was an insult when applied to an architect's blueprints. "Why?" I asked. "Because," he said, "it implies a level of fakery and a neglect of the third dimension. It implies that the work is scenographic, two-dimensional, flat."

I was reminded of why I like scenic designers who are also architects. It also reminded me why I like site-specific theater. And why I often think of design as subtext.

I remember once seeing my play *Eurydice* staged outdoors at Vassar. The actors were young. They were doing an honorable, virtuous job. And then, one day, it rained. And we could not rehearse outside. So the director, Davis McCallum, had them rehearse inside an old classroom building. He had them improvise blocking in relation to the architecture. Suddenly the performances went from being honorable to being full of genius. Orpheus wrote his letters to Eurydice on a giant chalkboard. When she followed him out of the underworld, she was on a real staircase, and we, the audience, all trooped behind.

Once the language was in the actors' minds, and their bodies were freed from blocking, and in relationship to real architecture, they became virtuosic. Metaphor suddenly had a more intimate relationship with reality. The actor was real, the staircase was real, the emotion was real, and the language floated on top.

93. Archaeology and erasers

Les Waters, my friend and collaborator, said the other day, "I'm worried." "Why?" I asked. "Because my daughter said she wants to be an archaeologist." "Oh?" I said. "Yes," he said. "Why is that bad?" I asked. "Because," he said, "it secretly means she wants to be a director." He said his childhood dream was to be an archaeologist, and that he knew many wonderful directors who likewise fantasized about digging in the dirt as children, hoping to be archaeologists, including Anne Bogart. I asked him what he thought the connection was between archaeology and directing. He said, "I think it's about finding out the invisible, buried structure of a thing. And if you are me, after you find the structure, you erase it." I gasped. I understood, newly, why I love it when Les directs my plays.

I remember once in third grade being asked to do a painting. I made a painting. I loved my painting. Then we were told to cover it in black paint so that we could scratch lines into the paint and make a design. I was horrified. I had made something beautiful, and I didn't want to cover it up.

The directors, designers, actors, and indeed writers I most admire have no problem with erasing their own work. I love directors who direct and say, Don't look at my directing, or designers who say, Don't look at my design, or actors who say, Don't look at my acting. So many directors find the structure of a play and then underline it with a bold marker. But what kind of bravery is required to find the structure of a play and then erase it?

If archaeology is uncovering a deep historical structure that can't be seen, and directing is uncovering an invisible structure buried in the play, then what is the difference between historical and narrative structure? Between fossils and narrative moments hidden in the sediment? And what of erasure and the unfinished? The compulsion to complete the historical narrative, or the theatrical structure, is deep. But I think of children, who dig in the sand, find a beautiful shell, look at it, see it fully, and then, rather than collect it, put it back.

94. On standard dramatic formatting

Why are stage directions generally in parentheses? If you (the playwright) want them treated as parentheticals, put them in parentheses, but if they are as important to you as the dialogue, as they are to me, do not put them in parentheses, and insist on using your own punctuation, as any novelist or poet would.

Punctuation is philosophy and rhythm in a play. Actors understand this. I think readers do too. And I think many more directors would begin to treat stage directions as visual speech rather than as filigree if they were not always hiding in parentheses.

95. On the Summer Olympics and moving at the same time

While breast-feeding twins, I watched the Summer Olympics, riveted by the opening ceremony in Beijing. The amount of virtuosity and coordination required was proof that the Chinese could effectively decimate most other nations, including ours. And yet in this case, the coordinated movement was used in the service of joy.

My older daughter asked me, "Mom, how can so many people move exactly at the same time?" And I said, "They practice." She watched, rapt. And I thought, Why is it so moving to see people move or dance at the same time? Thousands of people moving at the same time, in vaguely martial fashion, could mean: *We could kill you if we wanted to.* But instead we are moving our arms and legs at the same time to express joy, friendliness, and grace.

At the theater it is mesmerizing when people dance at the same time, sing at the same time, speak at the same time, or even walk at the same time. We know something has been rehearsed, or coordinated, when people move or speak simultaneously. And rather than being pained by the artificiality of moving or speaking at the same time, we often experience joy from the virtuosity of synchronization, from the always implied memory of a collective rehearsing together. And, I would argue, we experience joy and relief that such a potentially martial activity is being used to make us laugh instead of to make us die.

96. The first day of rehearsal

On the first day of rehearsal for my translation of *Three Sisters*, the director, John Doyle, pulled out a large costume rack, crammed with bustles, top hats, rehearsal skirts, rags, three-piece suits, dilapidated white wedding dresses, and sad sweaters. He instructed the actors to pick out whatever costume they thought their character might wear. The actors were giddy with excitement, suddenly young children, rushing to the costume rack.

Once the actors had changed into their costumes, John said, "Olga, where do you think you might sit?" Olga sat where she thought she might sit. "All right, Olga," said John, "begin the play." "What?" asked Alma, the actress playing Olga. "Begin the play," said John. And so Olga began the play. "Father died a year ago today, on your birthday, Irina . . ." I was so moved to see the actor begin simply, wearing a costume she'd chosen, and sitting in a spot she'd chosen.

Usually, a first day goes something more like this. The actors arrive. The entire theater staff arrives, occasionally along with some board members. We eat stale donuts and mill around nervously. The artistic director says a few words. The director does a presentation. The designers do a presentation. The playwright says some awkward heartfelt things. It's something like an ad campaign, but for who? We're still trying to convince the theater to do our play, but they're already doing it! We tell the actors how the play will look and sound, proud of our work, but because we've done the work already, the actors' very particular imaginations won't influence any of our big plans!

Then we sit down nervously, surrounded by a ring of about fifty people (depending on how big the theater is), and we read the play out loud at a table. The pencils are sharp, and the actors do a strange dance of auditioning for each other. The day ends, we are all relieved, and the next day we actually begin rehearsal. What if the first day of rehearsal could contain more joy? More costumes and fewer packets of information? What if it were as secretive and intimate as children building a fort, covering themselves with blankets, sitting in the dark, saying to the outside world: keep out, keep out, for now . . .

97. On watching *Three Sisters* in the dark

On the final run-through of *Three Sisters*, John Doyle ushered me into a dark rehearsal room. "Here's a torch," he said. "A what?" I asked. He handed me a flashlight and ushered me in.

The actors, he explained, had been rehearsing in the dark for the past two weeks. John said it made them self-conscious to rehearse in the light. This might well have been true. For the observer, though, the curious effect of not being able to *see* the actors was not being able to *hear* them. In other words, the senses blurred. As I watched the run-through, it appeared as though the actors were muttering in the dark, because I couldn't see them. I searched out the lighting designer afterward. "Jane," I said, "they won't be in the dark, in Cincinnati, will they?" "Oh no," she said, "at least not by opening night."

And I thought, What does it mean that in the theater illumination affects one's hearing, and sound affects one's sight? Paula Vogel maintains that theater is an experience of synesthesia, that is to say, the blurring of the senses. One of my favorite directors, Jessica Thebus, from Chicago, has synesthesia. For her, every number has a color. Every month has a color. It strikes me that directors with synesthesia are the proper people to direct plays or compose music. Duke Ellington, Leonard Bernstein, and Franz Liszt all had synesthesia. Ellington once said, "If Harry Carney is playing, D is dark blue burlap. If Johnny Hodges is playing, G becomes light blue satin." How to make sound visible, how to give sound color?

I remember being in a parking lot with Jessica Thebus in Chicago while she was directing my play at the Goodman Theatre. The parking lot assigned each floor a number and a color. Jessica and I wandered the parking lot and she said, "We can't be on Four Yellow, clearly, because the number four is intrinsically blue." And I thought, My play is in very good hands.

98. The audience is not a camera; or, how to protect your audience from death

Walter Benjamin argued years ago in "The Work of Art in the Age of Mechanical Reproduction" that actors would begin to act for cameras and not for audiences.

Recently, I was doing a play at a loft in Brooklyn called the Invisible Dog. The designer thought it might be a good idea to transport the whole audience on risers the whole length of the warehouse at a pivotal moment, without telling them we would do so. The effect would be like a camera suddenly creating a long shot. Everyone thought this was a cool idea. (With a sinking feeling, I remembered Anne Bogart once telling me to regard with suspicion any idea that seems cool.)

At any rate, our guerrilla gang went about figuring out how to make a mechanism that would move the entire audience back suddenly on a riser. With some engineering, some favors, and some luck, our small and merry band created a riser that could in fact move the entire audience the length of the loft. We were jubilant in tech. We all sat on the riser, and suddenly we were far away! It was joyful! It was surprising. It was cool.

The next morning I checked my e-mail, and Lucien, the proprietor of the Invisible Dog, had written to me something like: "What a thing you have made! I only hope it doesn't go through the holes in the floor, eh?" (Yes, his e-mail had a French accent.) "What holes in the floor?" I wrote back. "Come, I will show you today," he said. Sure enough, there were holes in the floor. You could see all the way from our third-floor loft clear into the second-floor loft. I had visions of the riser moving, and suddenly a crack of wood, and our audience members falling through the floor to their deaths on top of the artists who worked on the second floor, killing them also. I, as the acting artistic director, said, "Guys, I don't think we can move sixty live bodies and however many tons of machinery over an old floor with holes in it. I don't think it's very safe." "But we did all the calculations," they said. "But you can see the floor below in little holes in the wood," I said. "But our blocking and design is based on this concept," they said. "But people could die," I said. "No risers."

No one (with the possible exception of the technical director) was very pleased about the change. We reblocked the entire second act in one night, and I found I much preferred it without the conceptual move. We were no longer proceeding as though the audience were a camera, capable of being pulled back, through automation, to create a long shot.

I think that in the contemporary theater we don't consciously think of our audience as an inanimate mechanism, but as digital media are more and more in our lives, we more and more imagine the audience as a camera and design as something to be photographed. This gives theater a strange gloss, a strange preening quality as though it were about to be photographed. Whereas its charm is its very human gaze. I derived a few first principles from this experience:

1. The audience is not a camera.
2. Be suspicious of cool ideas.
3. Don't ever, ever kill your audience.

99. On endings

I do not like to end my plays with the phrase "End of Play,"
even though editors often cross out "The End" and substi-
tute the phrase "End of Play." To me "The End" signifies
mythic time and the notion that, oddly, there is no end.
"The End," for me somehow implies its opposite. Its very
finality implies a new cycle beginning. Whereas "End of
Play" implies the end of some aesthetic object that has a
definite and real end because it is, after all, only an object.
Why does "End of Play" make me sad, whereas "The End"
seems triumphant? Daring, even?

I love how *The Bald Soprano* ends with its own beginning. I once saw a twenty-four-hour version of the play in
the New York International Fringe Festival. The play began
as soon as it ended, over and over, for a complete twenty-
four-hour cycle. The audience could come back and see the
play at 4:00 a.m., when the wigs were coming unglued and
the irrational was gaining.

There is a natural dread of endings. One wants to feel as though endings contain beginnings, in spite of, or perhaps because of, their finality. But are we becoming inured to the idea of cyclical time now that we rely less and less on clocks and more and more on digital devices that have a linear progression? We no longer see time going in a circle, we see it marching forward ceaselessly, soundlessly . . . And if we fail to perceive time as cyclical, is time itself becoming less cyclical, insofar as time is partially a matter of perception?

When did people start writing "End of Play" rather than "The End"? Of course in the Renaissance they could end their plays "Exeunt" (or rather a typographer did years later), or they could write epilogues in rhyming verse. Years later they wrote "Curtain," but we don't generally have curtains or rhymes or epilogues anymore, so we have to write that sad little phrase, "End of Play." Oh, dear. "End of Play" has me sighing on my pillow. "End of Play" has me never beginning again.

100. On community theater

My mother directed *Enter Laughing* at the Wilmette Community Theater when I was eight years old. I came to every rehearsal, and I was crushed when the run ended. Harry Teinowitz, an awkward young actor with a lisp, played David, the hapless would-be actor, who walks into an audition and, reading literally from the script, says, "Enter laughing." I found the actress who played Angela Marlowe horribly, painfully glamorous, both on stage and off—the slow way she put on her stockings in her dressing room, and the way she would smoke on her breaks. So I was given this early sense that there was a halo of glamour around theater, even at the Wilmette Community Theater, where dentists played heroes and businessmen played dentists.

I took notes in the back, in the dark of the theater, and gave them to my mother, who often passed my notes on to her actors. (This formative experience might make me trying to directors even now.) I saw almost every performance of *Enter Laughing*, and when I learned that my mother and father were going to closing night and my sister and I were to be left home with a sitter, I felt wretched and betrayed. I cried on the floor of the living room, bereft, as my mother and father walked out the door. Not only had I seen it for the last time, I didn't know I'd seen it for the last time, so hadn't properly savored and mourned the final experience.

The second production that was etched into my young mind was of *A Midsummer Night's Dream* at Regina Dominican High School, a Catholic school run by nuns, also directed by my mother. She set it in the 1920s; the rustics were gangsters, and the fairies were flappers.

I came to tragedy later. *Romeo and Juliet* at North Shore Community Theater; my mother played the nurse, directed, as I recall, by the grand pooh-bah of North Shore Community Theater, a rotund theatrical man with a beard and a booming voice, named Ron Tobas. Every night my mother howled in grief over the apparently lifeless body of her charge. It was strange to see my mother howl in grief. "My lamb! My lady!" as she collapsed over a body. I had dreams, as a twelve-year-old, that I had to go on as Juliet. And when I cried at the play, I cried for Juliet, but more, I cried for my mother crying for Juliet. Which perhaps gave me a displaced point of view, of who the main character might actually be in a tragedy.

These formative productions weren't necessarily the best, in the professional sense of the word. They were born of small communities—a high school and a straight-up *community theater*—one of the most detested compound words in the annals of professional theater. But I was affected by seeing work born of people I was related to or knew casually. What is more moving than seeing someone you love on stage, or, better yet, watching someone watch a beloved person on stage? The watcher is lit up, transformed.

Why do people go to plays anyway? Perhaps because they played the angel in their church Nativity play, or because they played Clarence Darrow in high school, or because their mother sewed costumes, as did Peachy Taylor, who made all the costumes for the North Shore Community Theater. And why do we go to community theater? Not because the reviews were good, but because *we have to*—because the person we know who is involved would be *offended* if we didn't—we go, in other words, because of the social contract. The ticket prices are minimal or nonexistent. The contract that binds the audience to the work is nonmaterial and not terribly aesthetic; it is based on social ties. The play is an occasion to exercise and celebrate social bonds rather than the other way around.

It seems somehow significant to me that after all the beautiful professional productions I've seen of Paula Vogel's work, it was a student production of *The Baltimore Waltz*, inside a black box that used to be a university cafeteria that was later shut down because of asbestos on the ceiling— it was *this* production of her work that still moves me to tears when I think of it. And remembering such productions reminds me that the theater cannot be reduced to once-a-month luxuries for professionals. Play itself is a primary process, not a luxury, not a hobby, but something all children must do to survive into adulthood.

When I watch my children play, and they are at one moment a self-proclaimed mean turtle and then a nice turtle and then a grown man, each fiercely and completely, it reminds me of the primary human hope that identity might in fact be fluid, that we are simultaneously ourselves and the beasts in the field, a donkey, a queen, a starlet, a lover—and that identity might be nothing more than dipping our Heraclitean feet in the river, moment to moment. And if identity is fluid, then we might actually be free. And furthermore, if identity is fluid, then we might actually be connected—in Whitman's sense—if we can be the leaves of grass and also the masses on the Brooklyn Bridge, then we can leave the ego behind and *be world* for a moment. And this is one reason why we go to theater, either to identify with others, or to *be* others, for the moment; and in what we call community theater, the identification might be stronger, because we are more likely to either play the donkey ourselves or know the donkey intimately.

I do not claim a general preference for community theater over and above professional theater; I spend more time these days in professional theater, which I suppose makes it my community. But what I mean to say is the productions that have had the biggest impact on me—have ferreted their way into the most porous, childlike parts of me, winnowed in, and stayed there—have also been the smallest in scale. Smallness is subversive, because smallness can creep into smaller places and wreak transformation at the most vulnerable, cellular level. In a time when largeness is threatening to topple us, I wish to remember and praise the beauty of smallness, in order to banish the Goliath of loneliness. So thank you, Paula, thank you to my mother and to Shakespeare, thank you to the Ron Tobases, Angela Marlowes, and Peachy Taylors, for making me less lonely in this terribly large world.

215

Acknowledgments

Many thanks to some early readers of these essays: Kathy
Ruhl, John Lahr, Todd London, Bruce Ostler, Lydia
Weaver, Julia Cho, and, always, Paula Vogel. To some later
readers of the essays: Nicholas Dawidoff, Mark Epstein,
Quill Camp, Max Ritvo, Katherine Schultz, Sarah Ful-
ford, Edward Carey, Sherry Mason, André Bishop, and
Anne Cattaneo. To Terry Nolan, who thought there was
enough here to make a book, I am eternally grateful. To
some early audiences of these essays when I read bits of
them out loud at Vassar, Franklin & Marshall, University
of Scranton, Washington University, University of Colo-
rado, and the Michener Center. To the collaborators who
made their way into these essays: Les Waters, Anne Bogart, Mark Wing-Davey, John Doyle, Davis McCallum,
Jessica Thebus, Michael Cerveris, Laura Benanti, Maria
Dizzia, and Roy Harris. For Martha Karess, who sup-
ported me so wonderfully during bed rest. And I am very

grateful to Jonathan Galassi; to Mitzi Angel, a brilliant and passionate minimalist; and to Will Wolfslau.

Also, thanks to Tina Howe, who has given me courage in life and art many times over. Tina gave me my first good-luck charm for an opening night when I was twenty-six. When I first had the twins, she visited me and took me out of the house and said, "Sarah, soon they will be in school! I still hear an alarm bell every day at 3:00 p.m., and I stop writing then! But 9:00 a.m. to 3:00 p.m. are perfect hours for a writer! And until they are in school, enjoy rolling around the floor with them! It all goes very fast." And my friend Kathleen Tolan, a brilliant playwright and mother of two, was one of the first people I called when I learned that I was pregnant with twins. I burst into tears on the phone with her, and she said, "Don't worry! Big families are wonderful! And I will help you!" And so she did.

Perhaps it would hearten me to name some of the play-wright mothers who give me inspiration: Julia Cho, Diana Son, Lynn Nottage, Rinne Groff, Theresa Rebeck, Julia Jordan, Jenny Schwartz, Tanya Barfield, Marsha Norman, Amy Herzog, Beth Henley, Kate Marks, Karen Hartman, Bridget Carpenter, Elizabeth Egloff, Quiara Hudes, Suzan-Lori Parks, Caryl Churchill, Adrienne Kennedy, and Karen Zacarías.

To my children, Anna, William, and Hope, who make brief appearances in these essays. And to my husband, always, for making the writing life along with family life possible, and good. To a big-tent circus love.

A Note About the Author

Sarah Ruhl's plays include *In the Next Room, or the vibrator play* (Pulitzer Prize finalist; Tony Award nominee for best new play); *The Clean House* (Pulitzer Prize finalist, 2005; winner of the Susan Smith Blackburn Prize); *Passion Play: a cycle* (PEN American Award); *Dead Man's Cell Phone* (Helen Hayes Award); and, most recently, *Stage Kiss* and *Dear Elizabeth*.

Her many plays have been produced on Broadway, off-Broadway, regionally throughout the country, and internationally. They have been translated into more than fifteen languages, including Polish, Russian, Korean, and Arabic.

Originally from Chicago, Ruhl received her M.F.A. from Brown University, where she studied with Paula Vogel. Ruhl has since been the recipient of a MacArthur Fellowship, the Helen Merrill Emerging Playwright Award, the Whiting Writers' Award, the PEN/Laura Pels International Foundation for Theater Award for a mid-career playwright, a Feminist Press's Forty Under Forty Award, and the 2010 Lilly Award. She is currently on the faculty of the Yale School of Drama and lives in Brooklyn with her family.